MW01268101

MONKEYS DON'T WEAR
SILVER SUITS

Kelly's Little Green Men
& the 2017 Total Solar Eclipse

Tim Ghianni
Rob Dollar

PUBLISHED BY WESTVIEW, INC.
KINGSTON SPRINGS, TENNESSEE

ii

PUBLISHED BY WESTVIEW, INC.
P.O. Box 605
Kingston Springs, Tennessee 37082
www.publishedbywestview.com

ISBN 978-1-62880-020-3

First edition, January 2014

Good faith efforts have been made to trace copyrights on materials included in this publication. If any copyrighted material has been included without permission and due acknowledgment, proper credit will be inserted in future printings after notice has been received.

The authors intend to donate a portion of the proceeds from some of the direct sales of this book to the Kelly Community Organization.

All photos from the authors' personal collections.

Printed in the United States of America on acid free paper.

October 9, 2013

DEDICATION

Mark Twain once said, *"Truth is more of a stranger than Fiction."* With this thought in mind, the authors dedicate this book to those courageous people in this world, who throughout their lives, unselfishly pursue, accept and embrace The Truth, wherever it takes them.

TABLE OF CONTENTS

FOREWORD

The authors of this book can't claim—in good conscience—to have ever seen a UFO or chased and fought with little men from the far corners of outer space—silver, green or any other color.

Then again, neither of us has ever eyeballed or held in our hands the "bug" that makes you sick to your stomach or gives you a cold. But, nonetheless, it exists…It's there, and no one with a brain questions it.

The same argument holds up for God, Our Heavenly Creator, of course. At least that's the way we figure it.

On a hot, clear summer night—Sunday, August 21, 1955—a flying saucer supposedly landed in Kelly, Kentucky, near a farmhouse occupied by eight adults and three children. What followed was described as a night of terror as the farm family engaged in an hours-long gun battle with gremlin-like space creatures that floated and were immune to bullets.

The legendary Kelly Green Men case, with its Close Encounter of a Third Kind, is considered the Granddaddy of UFO sightings, and many believe the pop culture phrase "Little Green Men" caught fire and spread with this fantastic tale.

Not that it matters that the space creatures actually were silver or metallic in color, at least according to those who did battle with them.

In all the years since the out-of-this-world beings came to visit, no one has been able to prove—or disprove, for that matter—the story told by the Sutton-Lankford family.

And, maybe, just maybe, that's a good thing.

Not knowing beyond a reasonable doubt most certainly is the reason the story of the Little Green Men of Kelly probably will live forever in the imaginations of people all over the Earth who look up at the sky every night... and wonder what—if anything— is out there in the blackness of this great big Universe ... and beyond?

Since man first walked the Earth, there always have been reports of strange, unexplainable objects in the sky.

Famous people in history are among the ranks of UFO believers...The distinguished list includes the late CBS television broadcaster Walter Cronkite, who once was known as "The Most Trusted Man in America."

Cronkite believed he saw a disc-type aircraft not of this world back in the 1950s. Luminaries including John Lennon, President Jimmy Carter, astronaut Buzz Aldrin and even Christopher Columbus reported their own UFO encounters.

Maybe there are those who might scoff at Lennon's reported encounter in the 1970s with four bug-like creatures with big bug eyes that were "scuttling around like roaches" according to John's friend Uri Geller. They probably wonder why John picked four bug-like creatures...Roaches or beetles ... or Beatles, perhaps?

But who can question Jimmy "I'll Never Tell A Lie" Carter and Uncle Walter? And who among us knows the final frontier of space as well as the second man to set foot on the moon? As for Columbus, if he could discover America, why not life from another planet?

Readers of this book will find that, although written in 2013, it offers a thoughtful glimpse into the very near future in the first and last chapters—thanks, in part, to poetic license and the strength of some mighty powerful imaginations.

Now, there's no smoking ray-gun in our book, so don't look for one. The authors have researched the Kelly case thoroughly and scrutinized a variety of theories offered over the years to try and explain that terrifying night more than a half-century ago. Commentary, criticism, humor and parody play a big part in our presentation of this amazing story.

Everything we've discovered about the Kelly incident is being thrown against the Wall of Skepticism to see just what sticks.

But, there's no doubt in our minds—described as "disturbed" by some folks who know us—that SOMETHING happened that night in Kelly.

But what?

The 62nd anniversary of the Kelly incident will be celebrated on Monday, August 21, 2017, which just so happens to be the date for a solar eclipse—the first with a path of totality crossing the United States' Pacific coast and Atlantic coast since 1918.

The 2017 eclipse also will be the first total solar eclipse visible from the United States since 1991, when the spectacle was seen from parts of Hawaii, and the first visible from the contiguous United States since 1979.

Ironically, a slice of Christian County, Kentucky, located northwest of Hopkinsville and very near the Kelly alien invasion site, will be at or near the epicenter of the 2017 total solar eclipse.

On the day in question, shortly before 1:30 p.m., the moon will pass between the Earth and the sun, totally obscuring the image of the sun for viewers in Western Kentucky.

The eclipse will be "greatest" in a rural area not far from Kelly and Hopkinsville, and when it occurs, the early-afternoon sky will turn pitch black for about 2 minutes and 40 seconds.

Will the so-called Little Green Men come back that day?

Let's hope it won't be too dark to see.

4

Co-authors Tim Ghianni (left) and Rob Dollar sit on a bench
at Founders Square in downtown Hopkinsville, Kentucky,
wearing shades as they think about the future.

Chapter 1
(Rob)

FIRING UP THE TIME MACHINE

Me 'n' old Flapjacks sat on a bench at Founders Square in downtown Hopkinsville, Kentucky, drinking our morning coffee.

It was hot. Boy was it hot.

Of course, in late August, during the Dog Days of Summer, the weather is always hot and muggy in "Hoptown," the affectionate—and appropriate—nickname for a railroad town where people once hopped on and off trains at all hours of the day and night back in the good, old days.

The big parade through downtown had just ended, and everyone was smiling mighty big while wiping the sweat from their brows. It had been a delightful parade with plenty of floats, marching bands, politicians and even clowns who were real clowns and not politicians.

While the weather might not have been unusual, what was going to happen later on this particular day—Monday, August 21, 2017—for sure would be most highly unusual. More unusual than a blue moon of Kentucky that was really blue or a Derby mint julep without bourbon.

Life as we know it was about to change, maybe forever, shortly before 1:30 p.m. Course there were those who said nothing would—or should—happen, but, we reckoned, they were gridlock-loving crackpots. Or members of the Tea Party. Flap liked to call these kind of people who hate even the thought of progress or a good time "The American Taliban," a term he picked up from watching *The Newsroom* TV show.

But that's an aside. Flap and I had been waiting patiently for this "happening" since the shaky days of the "Fiscal Cliff" and the second coming of "Saint Bill" Clinton, who somehow had slickly shed the image of huckster and philanderer to find himself in an unprecedented spot as much more than the grand old man of American politics. These events, of course, occurred many, many years after Korporate Amerika tossed us out of the newspaper profession for our humanity and senses of humor. No we hadn't been sitting on this bench the whole time, but now that we were wise senior citizens we KNEW something big was going to happen this very afternoon. So big that it was worth missing our naps.

Now, the whole world—skeptics, believers, poets, pickers, prophets and preachers—would soon be watching the Greatest Show on Earth, not just two old benchwarmers known as "The News Brothers"—Tim "Flapjacks" Ghianni, and me, Rob "Death" Dollar, a pair of damn nice guys loved by everyone in America except the crooks on Wall Street and the aforementioned American Taliban.

We were inspired. There we sat on that downtown bench, two old pals in all of our glory, wearing our handy trademark shades and literally warming up for a trek out to the country in a few hours to watch it all unfold.

The City of Hopkinsville had the welcome mat out all over town. Signs and marquees expressed the goodwill... "Howdy Visitors".... "Never Stop Exploring"... "Hoptown: The Final Frontier".... "Sunglasses For Sale." The Verizon store on Fort Campbell Boulevard really went hog wild with an "E.T. Phone Home" banner splashed across the front of its building.

America's Captains of Industry were in high spirits on this red-letter day as greenbacks filled the cash registers, which were ringing with that tune so loved by the Chamber of Commerce. People from all over the world were seeing and experiencing Hoptown for the very first time. They were everywhere. Restaurants were full. All the quick-shop, self-serve fuel pumps were either busy or empty. Lines at the hybrid-vehicle recharging stations stretched down Fort Campbell Boulevard. Not a single vacant hotel room could be found anywhere in the immediate area. There were even some shoppers at the normally empty Bradford Square Mall. Hopkinsville was well on its way to swelling to three or four times its normal population of 33,000.

And, it was still early, with many more people on the way. Nearby Interstate 24, which passes about 10 miles south of the city, was jammed with cars coming up from Nashville, Tennessee. More than one NASA truck and a shiny SWAT-like SUV with a Department of Homeland Security decal, all Hoptown-bound, had been seen at an apparent rest stop, parked outside the Cat West, a gentlemen's club (using the term "gentlemen" loosely) down in Oak Grove, Kentucky. Let's not judge, here, folks. After all, Uncle Sam had issued their orders to experience some kind of close encounter or at least a bump in the night.

Spectators looking up to the sky saw scores of Blackhawk helicopters from the nearby Army post at Fort Campbell flying low over the city, crammed full of "Night Stalkers," Green Berets and "Screaming Eagles" from the 101st Airborne Division (Air Assault). The soldiers, with their war faces on and their legs dangling from the openings on both sides of every aircraft, were ready for any conceivable threat under the sun.

Seven miles away, in the Kelly community, the seventh annual Little Green Men Days Festival was gearing down so that festival-goers could watch The Big Show.

In downtown Hopkinsville, traffic was bumper to bumper at Ninth and Main. The hungry were making quick pit stops at Ferrell's Snappy Service on South Main Street, taking advantage of a good opportunity to satisfy their big appetites with breakfast or a bag full of those heavenly, onion-laced hamburgers. A few motorists were slowing almost to a complete stop so they could enjoy the daily street show of Hopkinsville's most famous citizen—"Bird Dog" (aka Steve Page), a rather unique fellow who barks at cars and meows at fine-looking women when he's not cutting grass for a living.

Flap, in particular, was either taken or taken aback by the sight of this barking man. "You know, I think Bird Dog's got it all figured out," he said, with a chuckle and his own little "Woof." Good thing there wasn't a fire hydrant nearby, I figured.

Across the street from our bench, we observed a reporter from the local morning newspaper—the daily that didn't publish daily anymore—plying his craft as he covered this most historic day. Most likely a seasoned veteran of the paper, just beyond puberty, he was doing it all…Tweeting, snapping photographs, videotaping the crowds and even sending Text alerts to readers still reading the newspaper.

Somehow the young scribe also found the time to interview a person or two before glancing at his latest-generation, solar-powered iPad to admire his work out there in cyberspace. In fact, since we looked like easy targets, two old guys sitting there on the bench, he rushed over to talk to us. It didn't take him long to realize he was now face-to-face with the most notorious of the old school outlaw journalists—The News Brothers. But, with the paper's Internet edition deadline fast approaching, it was too late to turn around and run and not send an update.

"Sir, may I ask you how you feel?" the kid asked Flap, with a shrug of his shoulders.

"You can't handle the truth," Flap snarled back, adding "My name is 'F-L-A-P-J-A-C-K-S.' Don't misspell it or I'll cancel my *Kentucky New Era* Internet subscription."   The kid sheepishly jotted that down on his reporter's pad and nervously backed away, almost tripping over Bird Dog.

The "thorough" interview drew a round of laugher from me 'n' Flap. Even Bird Dog stopped barking long enough to chuckle.

"I'll bet they sell THOUSANDS AND THOUSANDS of papers tomorrow," Flap predicted, with sarcasm and irony flavoring his voice. "NOT," I responded, with a knowing kind of laugh. "There sure won't be no REAL newspaper that people can read while holding it in their hands…That dog won't hunt because they don't put out a print edition of the paper on Tuesdays. And guess what day tomorrow is?"

"This is big, you know," said Flap, who always tries to see the good in everything and everybody. He thought about it for a minute. "Maybe they'll have a special edition."

"Yeah…When pigs fly," Bird Dog oinked, jumping right into his impression of Arnold the Pig from television's *Green Acres*.

For weeks, rumors were running rampant that the President of the United States was coming to Hopkinsville to see "IT"—and maybe even "THEM."

The "it" was the long-anticipated total eclipse of the sun. Now, as destiny would have it, one of the most perfect spots to observe and marvel over this rare celestial extravaganza was the outskirts of Hopkinsville, where those in the know claimed the sky later this day would turn dark for about 2 minutes and 40 seconds.

Scientists further promised the total solar eclipse would be "greatest" about 10 miles northwest of Hopkinsville off Princeton Road, near the historic Orchard Dale farm in the Bainbridge-Sinking Fork community of Christian County. Early preparations for the eclipse—folks actually booking hotel rooms and making travel plans—had gotten under way back when Obama was in his first term, people were still afraid of Osama bin Laden and Hillary was traveling the globe as secretary of state.

For more than five years, local tourism officials had promoted Christian County's connection to the 2017 eclipse, creating a Facebook page and Web site. They even thought up a catchy slogan that played off the Kentucky Derby's claim as the most exciting two minutes in sports.

Today's view of the eclipse from Christian County was being billed as "The Most Exciting 2 Minutes and 40 Seconds in Astronomy."

While the "it" was a sure thing, there still were many doubts about the "them" actually showing up for this once-in-a-lifetime heavenly celebration.

"Mr. Death, do you really think the president is coming to Hopkinsville to watch the eclipse?" Flap asked me, adjusting his shades and patting at his shirt pocket for a cigarette, even though he hadn't smoked in 30 years, give or take a decade.

"It depends on what the meaning of the word 'is' is," I joked. Gotta admit it didn't make much sense when I said it, but, like I said, it was hot and maybe I was on the fringes of heat stroke.

Still, I wasn't finished with my answer to Flap's question. "Not to worry," I continued. "If the president ain't got time for us, it won't really matter. Because you can bet your plaid shirt our old buddy Lamar Alexander will show up in town. He's everybody's hero. Before the government shutdown back in 2013, he got our Do Nothing-Congress to pass that important law that lets folks who like to fish....well...FISH. And, we both know Hoptown's just full of people who like to catch—and tell—whoppers."

My old newspaper crony smiled at my feeble attempt at humor.

"If Lamar comes today, I hope he doesn't wear his plaid shirt," Flap quipped. "Because if he does, he'll melt for sure."

Then, Flap hit me with THE question, the one in the back of everyone's mind on this great day in history. "What about THEM...the Little Green Men...Do you really think they're coming back?"

"They're coming...Just you wait and see," I answered, displaying the confidence of the guy who just learned he's going to be competing with a one-legged man in a butt-kicking contest. Especially if that one-legged man was slow and clumsy.

"How do you know?" Flap asked. Course he already knew the answer. He was just waiting for it....and baiting me.

"Because..." I said, "...Remember what Lonnie Lankford told us 12 years ago...Monkeys Don't Wear ...."

"SILVER SUITS!" Flap screamed, helping me finish my sentence. Old Bird Dog about fell over his lawn mower, startled by the jubilant—and loud—word exchange. He started barking. And whining.....

Then, without missing a beat, the strange fellow with the ferocious bark began dancing a jig in the streets of Hoptown.

"Look!" Flap yelled. "Bird Dog's doing 'The Monkey!'"

It was quite a sight.

Now, other than "Never Trust a News Brother," the phrase "Monkeys Don't Wear Silver Suits" had been a part of our daily vocabulary for most of this new century.

It seemed quite logical to me that there most certainly would be Little Green Men for everyone to see before this day was over. The little fellows from outer space just had to be on the same galactic schedule as the total solar eclipse. You only had to take a look at history to glow with optimism.

Flap and I, back in the day when we were hotshot newspapermen, licensed to carry a notepad and pen and ask questions, had thoroughly investigated a legendary Hopkinsville-area UFO case involving our pal Lonnie Lankford.

Sixty-two years earlier on this very date in history but on a Sunday and not a Monday—and at night and not during the daytime hours—a farm family (the Sutton-Lankford clan) and some friends claimed a flying saucer filled with space creatures had landed near their house in Kelly, a pastoral (except for that night) village just north of Hopkinsville.

What followed was a night of terror that included an hours-long gun battle, but no bodies or any other solid evidence of creatures from another planet.

Too fantastic and unbelievable to be true? Who's to say…Something out of the ordinary apparently happened, but what?

The coincidence that a total solar eclipse would occur on the 62nd anniversary of the alien invasion just couldn't be a coincidence, I reasoned, because just the thought of it made the hair on the back of my neck stand up. Yes, smartasses, the back of my neck is one place where I still have hair.

The closeness of the eclipse's best-viewing site in Christian County to the town of Kelly—less than 10 miles "as the crow flies"—was another fact that startled me.

It was the Kelly Green Men story that put Kelly—and Hopkinsville, as well—on the world map. And, as the legend spread over the decades, it eventually led Hollywood director Steven Spielberg to study the August 21, 1955, incident and later become a rich man by making his unforgettable movie masterpiece, *E.T. the Extra-terrestrial.*

For true believers, there was no doubt about the Kelly incident. In the years after this much-heralded Close Encounter of the Third Kind (which, of course, later became another Spielberg film title) and in the countryside off Old Madisonville Road not too far from the almost "perfect" total-eclipse-watching spot, the focus had long since shifted to the question of WHEN would the space creatures make a return visit to Earth to finish their business? Whatever that business was.

"Probably coming back to terrorize ol' Lonnie again," Flap theorized, only half-joking, because he didn't know whether the time had come to get serious. What we both knew, for a fact, was that our good friend was one of the few who actually had some first-hand knowledge of that night of terror in Kelly and the little guys in the silver suits.

Sixty-two years to the day after their last visit....

It seemed perfectly logical that this would be the day for the Kelly spacemen to rocket back to Planet Earth, what, with the solar eclipse and all that hubbub going on. Besides that, why not show up today? The whole world, other than perhaps North Korea, was waiting...and watching.

Now, before we go any further, it should be noted the good people of Hopkinsville—a town founded when a tavern was carved out of the wilderness in 1796 —are a different breed. They're proud, hardworking, independent and sometimes full of it. Don't ask me to tell you what the "it" is. You can probably figure that out on your own. Some folks have never left the city limits in their entire lives. Many of them are convinced that their community, located in the fertile farm fields of Western Kentucky, was, and always will be, "The Center of the Universe."

To be sure, it always seemed like everything, and anything, of significance that happened in the world somehow had a connection to Hoptown.

There was more than ample "proof" to argue and defend the claim.

Why strangers, don't you know?

❖ Jefferson Davis, the only president of the Confederacy, was born just nine miles east of Hopkinsville, with his birthplace becoming the site of a state park featuring a monument that is the tallest concrete obelisk in the world.
❖ The infamous "Trail of Tears" passed through Hopkinsville and Christian County in the late 1830s, with

two Indian chiefs—Fly Smith and Whitepath—meeting their Maker along the banks of the mighty Little River.

- ❖ Benjamin Brandon, a soldier from Hopkinsville who fought the war with the Indians in the 1870s, had the misfortune of taking his last breath on this Earth at the Little Big Horn while serving with George Armstrong Custer.

- ❖ Edgar Cayce, one of the world's greatest psychics, lived the early years of his life in Hopkinsville and is buried in Riverside Cemetery. A friend of presidents and known throughout the world, he was called "The Sleeping Prophet." To be sure, he's in a deep sleep now.

- ❖ Spiro Agnew, Richard Nixon's disgraced vice president, served his country as a young officer at the nearby Army post—then known as Camp Campbell—during World War II and is believed to have lived at a hotel in Hopkinsville. Some say he skipped out on the bill.

- ❖ Just months after World War II ended, "Old Blood & Guts"—Army Gen. George S. Patton Jr.—was killed in an automobile accident in Germany. The tragedy only resulted in minor injuries to the driver of his staff car—Horace "Woody" Woodring, a mild-mannered guy who sold used cars in Hopkinsville in his civilian life.

- ❖ Television bad guy "J.R. Ewing" of *Dallas*, portrayed by the late actor Larry Hagman, may have been conceived in Hopkinsville, where his mother, Broadway actress Mary Martin, and father Ben Hagman were married in November 1930. Don't know if they stayed at the same hotel as Spiro, but I do know Mary Martin once played the role of "Peter Pan," the kid who refused to grow up, on Broadway.

- ❖ Cassius Clay/Muhammad Ali's grandparents—John and Eliza Grady—made their home in Hopkinsville in the early 1960s when "The Greatest" claimed the world heavyweight boxing championship by knocking out Sonny Liston with The Phantom Punch.

❖ Hopkinsville native Alvin Hugh "Jerry" Giles Jr. might be called the "Man in the Moon." Giles was one of the chief engineers of the engine that helped the Apollo manned space program's lunar module land safely and softly on the moon. His name—and those of everyone else on the development team—is etched on the part of each of the lunar modules that were left on the moon during the 1960s and 1970s.

❖ The Lone Ranger (the late actor Clayton Moore) visited Hopkinsville in January 1983, wearing sunglasses instead of his familiar black mask. It was the beginning of a lifelong friendship between The Lone Ranger and The News Brothers. Or if not, it should have been.

William T. Turner, the longtime historian of Hopkinsville and Christian County, was the clever fellow who championed "The Center of the Universe" theory and later christened it "The Hoptown Connection." Turner's enthusiastic pitch always seemed to convince even the most hardcore of the doubters: "Divine providence decreed that anything important in the history of the world has a direct connection with Hopkinsville and Christian County."

Funny, but when Flap first heard William espouse his theory of Divine Providence and Hopkinsville's role in everything important in the history of the world back in the late summer of 2005, he pulled me aside and whispered, "I wonder what Jesus thought when he used to visit Hopkinsville?"

He didn't dare ask William that question, though, because he actually was afraid the esteemed historian with the gift of gab would have an answer.

Regardless, even with an occasional flaw in the theory, local folks had more than enough permission to act serious as a heart attack whenever they joked and played mind games with strangers who dared to challenge the community's special relationship with the universe.

Flap, who first unearthed the "Monkeys Don't Wear Silver Suits" reasoning in a rather memorable newspaper interview with Lonnie Lankford, actually was a true believer that something big was going to happen on this day in Christian County. Maybe it was because he had spent too much time with me over the years. Or maybe it was the heat playing tricks on his mind.

The more we talked about it the more we convinced ourselves that everything made perfect sense to us as we sat on our bench on this hot August morning, watching the sea of humanity in Hoptown and making fun of Bird Dog.

The aliens definitely were returning to Earth, and they probably would find their way back to Christian County by searching out key navigational points like Land Between the Lakes, the Jefferson Davis Monument and the Wal-Mart Supercenters.

While we were deep in thought on our bench, my old boss and longtime friend, former Hopkinsville Mayor Rich Liebe, stumbled upon me 'n' Flap.

"Mr. Spaceman: Come on Down!" Rich sang, in his perfect *Price is Right* announcer's voice before he roared off on his Harley. "God Bless us all…Extra Good," he hollered, his voice echoing back to us from somewhere off in the distance.

The Little Green Men, if they ever had planned a follow-up visit, just had to pick TODAY for their return to Christian County and the greater "Hoptropolis" area—otherwise known as "The Center of the Universe."

The world as the naysayers saw it probably was going to come crashing down sometime later this afternoon…"THEY" were coming back. That was our story, and we were sticking to it.

"He who laughs last, laughs best," I barked, giving Flap a Thumbs-Up.

Removing his shades, he growled, offered up a wink and reached to his feet to retrieve his Styrofoam cup of coffee. He then dumped about half of it down his throat. It was hot. Boy was it hot.

A well near this bird bath in front of a doublewide trailer home on Old Madisonville Road in Kelly, Kentucky, is all that is left of the old Sutton-Lankford farm, supposedly visited by little men from outer space more than a half-century ago.

VISITORS IN THE NIGHT

The Kelly Green Men case has been the subject of numerous books, television documentaries and heated arguments for more than a half-century.

UFOlogists around the world, to this very day, regard this particular Close Encounter of the Third Kind as one of the most significant and investigated cases in the history of UFO incidents.

The story, no doubt, at face value, is out of this world. In a nutshell, a flying saucer is said to have landed in a field near a farmhouse in Kelly—a rural community about seven miles north of Hopkinsville, Kentucky—during the early evening hours of Sunday, August 21, 1955. With the discovery, the occupants of the farmhouse, 11 members of two families, engaged in an hours-long gun battle with—according to newspaper accounts of the time— between 12 and 15 space creatures that apparently were immune to bullets.

When the dust finally settled, there was plenty of chaos, but there were no bodies, alien or otherwise. Nor blood. Just some angry and frightened folks who told authorities, neighbors and newsmen the details of the attack.

Although the aliens were described by witnesses as silver in color, the already amazing tale, at some point, apparently was embellished by a creative soul at some newspaper somewhere. Since the encounter occurred in Kelly (as in Kelly green), the creatures should be "Little Green Men" in order to sell more newspapers.

It may have been one of the earliest references to Little Green Men, and the cleverness became responsible for forever shaping the narratives of future UFO cases, which almost invariably had the aliens described as being green.

Not surprisingly, as fate would have it, the Kelly UFO encounter would grow into the perfect legend over the years: No one could ever prove it actually happened. But, no one has ever been able to disprove the strange and frightening tale either.

Spending 20 years as a reporter and editor at Hopkinsville's then-daily newspaper—the *Kentucky New Era*—helped convert me into a Little Green Men junkie and self-professed know-it-all on what some people might consider the Granddaddy of UFO cases. Of course, I really didn't know everything about the Kelly incident, just enough to be dangerous and hold my own while arguing about it.

During my newspaper career, I participated in many assignments on the Kelly Green Men incident, including the time, in mid-April 2000, when a handful of us at the *Kentucky New Era*—George McCouch, Skip Aldridge, Lynn Gold and me—assisted a French UFO investigator with his examination of the case.

Heck, Yann Mege and his companion—Claudine Jung—spoke better English than most of the residents of Hopkinsville, so there certainly was no language barrier in our investigation of the UFO case known throughout the world.

Prior to August 1955, there already had been a few published reports in the UFO world about "little men" and even "green" Martians. But Mege told us he believed the "Little Green Men" phrase went viral and gained world-wide fame as a result of the Kelly case.

Based on his field investigation, the Frenchman wrote at least one article that was published in June 2001 in a French magazine ("Kelly: la nuit des extraterrestres," *Phénomèna, N°45*). Maybe he followed through with his plans to write a book. I don't really know.

Now, I can't read French any better than I speak it (I don't), but I'm told Mege discovered that some of the farmhouse occupants had access to science-fiction reading material and had heard stories about other UFO sightings. Mege even claimed that Billy Ray Taylor, who had lived in two states (West Virginia and Pennsylvania), where well-publicized UFO sightings had taken place prior to the Kelly incident, probably influenced the Sutton-Lankford family.

Furthermore, Mege pointed out that in the months before the little men made their appearance, at least five science-fiction and two fantasy movies supposedly were showing at movie-houses across the country, including at the six theaters and drive-ins in Hopkinsville.

The feature films had titles like *Conquest of Space* and *Flying Saucers*.

And, let's not forget it also was in 1955 that Frederic Brown published his best-selling science-fiction novel—*Martians, Go Home*. Interestingly, the dust-cover from the first edition actually featured an illustration that depicted Martians as...well... Little Green Men.

This fascination with flying saucers that swept across the country in 1955 apparently led Mege to conclude his investigation with the theory that the Kelly incident was nothing more than a hoax.

Renaud Leclet, another UFOlogist from France—a man I didn't have the pleasure of meeting or working with—also studied the Kelly case and in August 2001 theorized that the farmhouse occupants actually saw Eagle Owls that night, and for whatever reason, mistook them for space creatures.

Now, as a nosey newspaperman who's always been fascinated by the unknown, I couldn't help but learn a few things about the Kelly incident during my tenure at the Hopkinsville newspaper.

But more importantly, over the years, I worked very closely with many colleagues who knew the story from front to back cover, allowing me to absorb more of it. At the top of the list was the late Joe Dorris, a former *Kentucky New Era* editor and publisher. Joe was among the first reporters at the invasion scene the day after the 1955 incident. He wrote the initial front-page story that was picked up by newspapers and media outlets all over the world.

There was Mary D. Ferguson, a longtime *Kentucky New Era* reporter who was the wife of retired Kentucky State Trooper R.N. Ferguson. Trooper Ferguson helped investigate the alien encounter and became one of the most interviewed individuals in Kentucky as a leading skeptic of the case.

There was the late David L. Riley, another former editor-in-chief of the newspaper, who studied and wrote about the Kelly Green Men legend as a *Kentucky New Era* reporter and later, in the mid-1980s, presented a paper on it to the Christian County Historical Society.

And then there was Jennifer Pitzer Brown, who early in her *Kentucky New Era* reporting days, received what she believed was a veiled threat from the most dominant and forceful of personalities among the farmhouse occupants after she contacted him in order to work up an anniversary story on the legendary incident. Elmer "Lucky" Sutton, the emotionally-scarred eyewitness who later died at the age of 65 in December 1995, still was haunted by the experience and bitter because his family had been ridiculed for years. He wanted to be left alone, and he didn't want to see another story done on a subject that was a sore point for his family.

That wished-for end of Kelly incident stories wasn't going to happen in his lifetime or anyone's lifetime, for that matter. It's one of those stories that my old friend, Flap, tells me "has legs." It means it's basically of interest to everyone who ever looked at the sky at night and wondered what was up there.

In the time I was at the Hopkinsville newspaper, just about every month, someone from somewhere would show up at the front desk, asking questions about the Kelly Green Men case and wanting to view the newspaper's archives. The visitors were from all over the world. Sometime long before I arrived at the *Kentucky New Era* in December 1983, one of these inquiring minds, left alone with the valuable bound volumes of old *Kentucky New Era* issues, actually ripped out the front page containing the historical

Kelly story and got away while the getting was good. Thank God for microfilm.

After I learned about this dastardly deed, I mentioned it to Flap—then working at the Clarksville, Tennessee, newspaper—in an urgent telegram. Flap was outraged, and he said the thief, if ever caught, should be hung by his private parts. Old Flap, you see, has a love affair with old-fashioned newspapers (the kind that they used to print on a press, anyway) and such bad behavior really pisses him off. I'm sure, at the time of the incident, Joe Dorris, who later became a member of Kentucky's Journalism Hall of Fame, was pissed off, too.

Long after Joe retired, and up until the day he died in November 1999, he was still receiving telephone calls about the Kelly Green Men case.

If Helen was the face that launched a thousand ships, then it was Joe Dorris' August 22, 1955, front-page, above-the-fold newspaper story that sent the Kelly incident hurtling through the Universe where it will forever reverberate and capture people's imaginations.

The story, published the day after the alleged alien attack in the 5-cents afternoon edition of the *Kentucky New Era*, carried the following headline and sub-head:

"Story of Space-Ship, 12 Little Men Probed Today"
"Kelly Farmhouse Scene of Alleged Raid By Strange Crew Last Night; Reports Say Bullets Failed To Affect Visitors"

The story began: *"All kinds of investigations were going on today in connection with the bizarre story of how a space-ship carrying 12 to 15 little men landed in the Kelly community early last night and battled occupants of a farmhouse."*

Packaged with Dorris' story was a captivating photograph showing the farmhouse and two of the occupants who supposedly fought the space creatures—Elmer "Lucky" Sutton, who was seen holding a shotgun, and Billy Ray Taylor, who claimed his hair had been pulled during the attack by one of the little men, who at the time was perched on the small, overhanging roof.

THIS IS THE HOUSE near Kelly where little men from out in space were supposed to have been seen last night. With the gun is Lucky Sutton looking up at the porch roof where one of the invaders supposedly sat. In the doorway is Billy Ray Taylor, who says his hair was pulled by the man on the roof.

Story Of Space-Ship, 12 Little Men Probed Today

Kelly Farmhouse Scene Of Alleged Raid By Strange Crew Last Night; Reports Say Bullets Failed To Affect Visitors

All kinds of investigations were going on today in connection with the bizarre story of how a space-ship carrying 12 to 15 little men landed in the Kelly community early last night and battled occupants of a farmhouse.

Most official of the probes was

went out of the house to get a bucket of water. He saw what looked like a flying saucer come over the trees and land in a field at a point about a city block behind the house. There was no explosion, only a semi-hissing sound, and the watcher returned to the house with the bucket of water.

The report of a flying saucer and alien encounter in Kelly, Kentucky, in late August 1955, made the front pages of newspapers around the world. (Courtesy of *Kentucky New Era*).

Dorris visited the Kelly farmhouse the morning after the invasion, talked to family members and inspected the site where the flying saucer supposedly landed, according to David Riley's 1985 research paper on the Kelly Green Men case.

"They told me the imprint of the spaceship was visible in the field but people walking through the field had disturbed the imprint," Dorris told Riley in an interview.

Interestingly, a copy of Dorris' newspaper story would end up in the Air Force's Project Blue Book file on the Kelly incident about two years later.

On Monday, August 22, 1955, the day after the visit of the little men, the No. 1 song in America was *"Rock Around The Clock"* by Bill Haley and His Comets.

The alien invasion of Kelly wasn't the only thing of interest in that day's edition of the *Kentucky New Era*.

National news stories on the front page detailed the devastating and deadly flood in the Northeastern United States and President Eisenhower's plan to host a summit with the governors of the "flood-dazed" states. Riots in Morocco also killed 800 people, according to a below-the-fold story.

Local stories on the front page of the paper advised readers that two Fort Campbell soldiers riding on a motorcycle had been seriously injured the night before just outside of the Hopkinsville city limits when their bike collided with a car on U.S. 68-East, and Bethel College would be hosting a piano recital in its air-conditioned auditorium later that night featuring Hopkinsville native Marshall Butler of New York City.

The *Kentucky New Era*'s Society Page that day heralded the Sunday wedding at Ninth Street Christian Church of Elizabeth Vernell Thomas and Charles L. Sowell.

On the Sports pages, baseball lovers learned that Al Kaline of the Detroit Tigers still led the Majors in batting with a .351 average. The New York Yankees remained in first place in the American League, with Mickey Mantle homering and Don Larsen pitching a six-hitter for a 6-1 victory over the Baltimore Orioles on Sunday. Meanwhile, the slumping Brooklyn Dodgers, despite a 6-4 loss to the Philadelphia Phillies, also on Sunday, remained

24

atop the National League standings. Another sports story announced that popular welterweight boxer Chuck Davey planned to return to the ring after a 15-month layoff.

And then there were the advertisements in the August 22, 1955, issue of the *Kentucky New Era*. Subscribers discovered that *East of Eden* with James Dean, was playing that evening at the Skyway Drive-in, while the movie, *It Came From Beneath The Sea*, was scheduled to open Wednesday at the Alhambra Theatre. Would-be shoppers saw ads for Davy Crockett T-shirts, on sale for 25 cents apiece, at the John Green store at Main and 10th, and for the new V8-powered Dodge Custom Royal Lancer at the Bob Corum Motor Co. on Liberty Street. At Keach Furniture Co., General Electric washers were selling for $319.95.

The Classified section of that day's newspaper ran an ad for a house on Victory Drive, with a purchase price of $8,750.

This was the world as people knew it back in 1955, when Ike was president and things were good and booming for America's middle class, rebuilding their lives after the end of the Depression and World War II.

Now, it should be noted that, at the time of the Kelly incident, UFO reports were anything but unique in the United State, although claims of alien encounters were somewhat rare.

Only about eight years earlier, on July 7, 1947, the infamous Roswell UFO incident had made international headlines. That case, still the subject of controversy and conspiracy theories, involved an official government report that the military had recovered a spaceship with extraterrestrial life that had crashed on a ranch near Roswell, New Mexico. Within days, the story mysteriously changed, and the debris field on the ranch was attributed to a downed weather balloon.

Decades later, the Air Force again tried in vain to put the matter to rest with another story. Top brass publicly proclaimed that what was recovered near Roswell in 1947 actually was debris from a high-altitude surveillance balloon—manned with dummies—that had been part of a top-secret project undertaken during the Cold War.

Interestingly, just one week before the Kelly incident and only 80 miles north of Hopkinsville—near Evansville, Indiana— someone allegedly was attacked by a strange creature and nearly drowned while swimming in the Ohio River in a rural area where numerous people had seen strange lights in the summer sky.

If true, the victim—a 35-year-old woman—may have had a prior encounter with what would later be described as one of the "Hopkinsville Goblins," another name often used for the Kelly Green Men. The alleged attack occurred around twilight on August 14, 1955, while a group of friends went swimming in Dogtown, an area where "shiny objects" had recently been seen in the sky, according to published reports. The description of the gremlin-like creature in the river was very similar to the little men that supposedly showed up in Kelly the following weekend.

The Kelly Green Men incident has been investigated and debated for decades, and the general facts of the case are almost known by heart by anyone fascinated with UFOs and the unexplained.

Official documentation of the sensational story began just hours after the incident, and continued into the next day and following weeks. It later was reinforced with a thorough independent probe by Isabel Davis, a UFO investigator from New York City who showed up in Hopkinsville with her pen and notebook in the early summer of 1956—about 10 months after the alleged alien encounter.

A 1978 publication of the Chicago, Ill.-based J. Allen Hynek Center for UFO Studies (CUFOS), co-authored by Davis and Ted Bloecher, dissected and analyzed the facts and myths of the Kelly incident while putting it into context with other reported Close Encounters of the Third Kind that occurred in 1955. The 196-page report—*Close Encounter at Kelly and Others of 1955*—included interviews, maps, illustrations and photographs as well as materials obtained from the Air Force's Project Blue Book.

So what happened in Kelly, Kentucky, on that hot, clear August night in 1955?

Let's take a look at the information out there in the public domain, gathered over the years from published reports, CUFOS investigators, official documents and accounts given by witnesses, some of whom are now dead, and the others still living.

In 1955, about 150 people lived in the Kelly community. The scene of the epic battle with the space creatures was a one-story frame farmhouse—consisting of a kitchen and two rooms separated by a passageway or "dogwalk"—located on a three-acre tobacco and vegetable farm, about eight miles north of Hopkinsville off Old Madisonville Road. The home had electricity and a small electric refrigerator, but no indoor plumbing, radio, telephone or television. As for firearms, there were four in the house—two shotguns, a .22-caliber rifle and a pistol.

At the time of the attack, the home was occupied by eight adults and three children:

- ❖ Glennie Lankford, 50, who was twice a widow.
- ❖ Elmer "Lucky" Sutton, 25, Mrs. Lankford's son by her first deceased husband, Tillman Sutton.
- ❖ Vera Sutton, 25, wife of Lucky Sutton.
- ❖ J.C. (John Charley) Sutton, 21, another son from Mrs. Lankford's first marriage.
- ❖ Alene Sutton, 27, wife of J.C. Sutton.
- ❖ Lonnie Lankford, 12, Charlton Lankford, 10, and Mary Lankford, 7, the children of Glennie Lankford and her deceased second husband, Oscar Lankford.
- ❖ Billy Ray Taylor, 21, a West Virginia native, who had previously lived in Pennsylvania, and was in Kelly visiting with his friend, Lucky Sutton.
- ❖ June Taylor, 18, wife of Billy Ray Taylor.
- ❖ O.P. Baker, a Hopkinsville man in his early 30s, who was the brother of Alene Sutton and often stayed at the Sutton-Lankford house.

Lucky Sutton and Billy Ray Taylor, along with their wives, were employed by a traveling carnival, and they apparently were in Kelly visiting that particular weekend. Obviously Lucky was a proud carny—and proud of his nickname—if reports are true that he had the letters L-U-C-K-Y tattooed on the fingers of his left hand.

Not at the farmhouse on this fateful night were three other grown children from Glennie Lankford's first marriage, one of them a son named Frank Sutton...But NOT the same Frank Sutton, who about a decade later would become known to millions of Americans who watched the CBS television series, *Gomer Pyle U.S.M.C.*

Strangely enough, Frank Spencer Sutton, the actor immortalized for his role as Gunnery Sergeant Vince Carter, was born and raised about 26 miles away in nearby Clarksville, Tennessee, and would have been a grown man of 31 at the time of the Kelly incident. His parents were Frank Sims Sutton and Thelma Spencer Sutton.

Perhaps Kelly's Frank Sutton, who lived in Hoptown at the time, and the famous Frank Sutton—known for bellowing "I can't hear you!" at a befuddled Gomer Pyle—were distant cousins...Who knows?

On the night of the alien encounter, Sunday, August 21, 1955, around 7 p.m., Billy Ray Taylor, during a break in a card game, went outside to get a bucket of water from the nearby well. Away from the farmhouse, he observed something bright in the sky that he believed was a flying saucer. The spacecraft flew over the house and then landed in a ravine about 100 yards from the farmhouse.

Shaken to the core, Taylor retreated inside and immediately reported what he had seen in the night sky to the other occupants. Apparently, they thought Taylor, known for being a practical joker, was pulling a prank or maybe had just had his first experience with a shooting star. So no one really was alarmed by his story, and they laughed it off.

The mood changed around sunset, about 8 p.m., just as it was getting dark. The family dog began barking violently outside the farmhouse. Going to the back porch to investigate the commotion outside, Lucky Sutton and Taylor observed a strange glow approaching the farmhouse from the fields. At some point, the men realized the glow actually was a small creature, or creatures, that appeared able to float above the ground while coming toward them and the farmhouse.

The two men ran into the farmhouse, retrieved their weapons—a shotgun and .22-caliber rifle—and began shooting at the creatures, who were not affected in the least by the bullets that hit them. When hit, the creatures appeared to "flip" and then run off, disappearing into the darkness.

Even if they were not the world's best marksmen, the men from the farm surely had to inflict several of what should have been mortal wounds. After all, the fierce gun battle reportedly lasted for three or more hours, interrupted a few times by the dead silence of the night after the creatures seemingly disappeared from sight for a time.

But the battle continued to rage, resuming with the same intensity after at least two such periods of silence and inactivity, once when one of the creatures peered into a window, drawing immediate gunfire, and a second time when Billy Ray Taylor stepped outside on the porch and had his hair grabbed from above by one of the creatures as it sat on the small overhang from the roof.

In addition to Lucky Sutton and Taylor, Glennie Lankford and all but one of the adults in the farmhouse (believed to have been June Taylor) reportedly saw the space creatures at one point or another during the night.

The enemy "soldiers" were described as being about 3-foot-tall, with oversized heads; huge, luminous yellow eyes; big ears; long arms and big hands ending in talons. Silver or metallic in color, the little men appeared to float but they could also walk and run, and made absolutely no sound. The exact number of creatures involved in the attack ended up being one of the murky details that could not be firmly established from the questioning of the witnesses. All things taken into consideration, the alleged attack conceivably could have been the work of as few as a handful of the creatures and not the 12 to 15 reported in various media accounts.

Realizing it was futile to continue fighting the creatures, the occupants of the farmhouse loaded into two cars sometime around 11 p.m. and sped off to the police station in Hopkinsville, where they officially reported to everyone and anyone who would listen that they had been attacked by space creatures that had come out of a flying saucer.

Newspaperman David Riley, in his research paper for the Christian County Historical Society, recalled the late Deputy Sheriff George Batts' account of the two cars full of excited people roaring into town.

"We need help," Batts remembered one of them yelling. *"We've been fighting them for nearly four hours."*

R.N. Ferguson, then a young Kentucky state trooper, was home in bed when a state police dispatcher telephoned and told him to head to Kelly to investigate an incident involving a flying saucer and little men.

Riley's paper suggested Ferguson was not the least bit enthusiastic about responding to the call. *"I wasn't so skeptical that I wouldn't investigate it, but I wasn't expecting to shake hands with one of them, though,"* Ferguson quipped.

A motorcade of law enforcement officials—including Hopkinsville police officers, Kentucky State Police, Christian County sheriff's deputies and four military policemen assigned to nearby Fort Campbell—rushed out to the farmhouse to get to the bottom of whatever had happened.

That same night, apparently sometime between 6:30 p.m. and 11 p.m.—the exact time is unclear —a state trooper on duty near the Shady Oaks restaurant, some three miles from Hopkinsville and toward Kelly, observed what he believed were several meteors passing overhead. As the objects sailed through the night sky, the trooper reported hearing noises that he said were like exploding artillery shells. A variety of published reports suggest there also may have been several others in the Kelly community and surrounding areas who saw something unusual in the sky that night.

Were these objects in the night sky connected in any way to what happened at the Sutton-Lankford farmhouse? Or, were they just what they appeared to be—meteors?

It should be noted that the Perseid meteor shower, which has been observed for about 2,000 years, occurs during the months of July and August, with the peak of activity normally in mid-August.

When the army of law enforcement officials arrived at the Sutton-Lankford residence, they found evidence that guns had been fired inside and outside of the house, but there were no signs of space creatures, dead or alive, or solid evidence that a spaceship had landed in the vicinity. Nevertheless, there appeared to be common agreement that something had scared these people—scared them nearly to death.

Isabel Davis, in one of her summer of 1956 interviews with witnesses in the case, asked then-Hopkinsville Police Chief Russell Greenwell, now deceased, about his memories of that night in the Kelly countryside. He was among the lawmen who went to the scene to investigate the report.

"Something scared those people. Something beyond reason—nothing ordinary," Greenwell told Davis. The chief added that the family's attempt to seek help from the police in Hopkinsville was rather significant, in and of itself. *"These aren't the kind of people who normally run to the police for help. When they feel themselves threatened, what they do is reach for their guns."*

Greenwell recalled that something definitely was in the air that night when he and the other lawmen and investigators surveyed the site of the reported battle.

"In and around the whole area, the house, the fields, that night, there was a weird feeling," the chief noted. *"It was partly uneasiness, but not entirely. Everyone had it. There were men there that I'd call brave men, men I've been in dangerous situations with. They felt it, too. They've told me so."*

The biggest excitement as investigators checked out the scene came when one of the lawmen—a military policeman—stepped on a cat's tail while wandering around the property in the dark, and the cat let out a loud-pitched scream that broke the silence of the night.

"You never saw so many pistols unholstered so fast in your life," Greenwell said in the Davis interview. The cat apparently escaped unharmed, except for perhaps a sore tail.

Authorities departed the Kelly farmhouse sometime before 2 a.m. (now Monday, August 22, 1955), leaving the Sutton-Lankford family and their friends by themselves, alone with only their thoughts.

It wasn't long after the law left that the little men returned from seemingly nowhere, with Glennie Lankford, now in bed trying to go to sleep, spotting one of the creatures with his/her/its hands on the window screen of her bedroom. Lucky Sutton, alerted by his mother's screams, responded with a shotgun blast to the window frame. The battle was on…again.

A few more hours of what the farmhouse occupants already had experienced that night—sheer terror and frustration—followed. The last little man supposedly was seen sometime around 5:15 a.m. or about 30 minutes before sunrise.

Finally, everything was quiet at the farmhouse.

With the sun about to rise, the unwelcome visitors of the night had left the farmhouse and Kelly and apparently floated away to parts unknown in the solar system.

Would they come back?

With the new day, the Sutton-Lankford family soon had to deal with a problem involving new visitors: Hundreds and hundreds of curious sightseers who converged on the farm that day and the next, Tuesday, August 23, 1955.

"On Tuesday the Suttons put up a 'No Trespassing' sign, which did no more good than anything else since there was no way of enforcing the prohibition short of ringing the entire house and yard with policemen," Davis wrote in *Close Encounter at Kelly and Others of 1955.*

"That same day the Air Force issued two statements to the press: first, that there had been no official investigation of the reports of the spaceship and its passengers, and second, that there was no basis to the report."

The Air Force's Project Blue Book contains this sketch of one of the little men that supposedly landed in a flying saucer and attacked a farmhouse in Kelly, Kentucky. Although the creator of the sketch was not identified, it is believed to have been drawn by Andrew B. "Bud" Ledwith.

PROJECT BLUE BOOK

Before it shut down the "Project Blue Book" program, the Air Force investigated more than 12,000 UFO reports from 1947 to 1969.

The comprehensive study had two primary goals. First, and most importantly, the government wanted to determine whether UFOs (Unidentified Flying Objects)—whatever they were—posed a threat to national security. Secondly, scientists wanted to collect and analyze any UFO-related data or technology that might be useful to our country.

After an intensive scrutiny of the murky subject matter that lasted more than three decades, the plug officially was pulled on Project Blue Book on January 30, 1970. In terminating the program, the Air Force apparently concluded the UFO phenomenon was much ado about nothing. According to the top brass, most of the reported sightings over the years involved misidentifications of natural phenomena, like clouds or stars, or witnesses unable to recognize conventional or top-secret aircraft.

Nevertheless, there were some cases where the Air Force just couldn't put its finger on logical explanations.

So, while investigators ruled that the majority of the UFO sightings could be explained, they readily admitted there were around 700 "unidentified" cases in which they couldn't reach satisfactory conclusions.

The Center for UFO Studies (CUFOS), on the other hand, continues to insist there are more than 1,600 "unknown" UFO sightings in the Project Blue Book case files—including the Close Encounter of the Third Kind in Kelly, Kentucky, in August 1955.

With the end of Project Blue Book, thousands of UFO files were transferred from Wright-Patterson Air Force Base in Dayton, Ohio, to Maxwell Air Force Base in Montgomery, Alabama. By 1975, thanks to the declassification of the top-secret program, it became possible, under the Freedom of Information Act (FOIA), for ordinary citizens to obtain Xerox copies of any of the Project Blue Book documents.

Today, the National Archives in Washington, D.C., has custody of all Project Blue Book records relating to UFO investigations through 1969. Files are available for examination by the public in the research room of the archives' Military References Branch. There is also online access to the records.

In January 1985, the Air Force, likely hoping to forever distance itself from the thorny subject of UFOs, issued a final news release or "fact sheet" on its 1947-1969 Project Blue Book program.

It stated, in part: *"As a result of these investigations and studies and experiences gained from investigating UFO reports since 1948, the conclusions of Project Blue Book are: (1) no UFO reported, investigated , and evaluated by the Air Force has ever given any indication of threat to our national security; (2) there has been no evidence submitted to or discovered by the Air Force that sightings categorized as 'unidentified' represent technological developments or principles beyond the range of present-day scientific knowledge; and (3) there has been no evidence indicating that sightings categorized as 'unidentified' are extraterrestrial vehicles."*

The government news release continued: *"Since Project Blue Book was closed, nothing has happened to indicate that the Air Force ought to resume investigating UFOs. Because of the considerable cost to the Air Force in the past, and the tight funding of Air Force needs today, there is no likelihood the Air Force will become involved with UFO investigation again."*

The last paragraph of the "fact sheet" could probably make the hair on the back of a person's neck stand up: *"Periodically, it is erroneously stated that the remains of extraterrestrial visitors are or have been stored at Wright-Patterson AFB. There are not now nor ever have been, any extraterrestrial visitors or equipment on Wright-Patterson Air Force Base."*

Of course, no one should forget that the government, for decades, also denied the existence of Area 51 in the central Nevada desert. Then, out of the blue in August 2013, the CIA, in releasing documents on the U-2 spy plane program, acknowledged the facility, where scientists are believed to test intelligence tools and weapons.

Let's look at the Air Force's treatment of the Kelly Green Men case. It could well be true that Project Blue Book never "officially" investigated the Kelly incident, but that doesn't mean there was no interest in the case since Air Force officials apparently collected numerous documents and materials over the years.

Some people might be surprised to learn that Carl Sagan, the late and great astronomer, astrophysicist and author, actually looked into the Kelly Green Men Case.

In the mid-1960s, Sagan was a member of the Ad Hoc Committee to Review Project Blue Book, and on January 12, 1966, he wrote a letter to the Department of the Air Force in Washington, D.C.

The letter, which is part of the Project Blue Book Archive, referred to an upcoming meeting at Wright-Patterson Air Force Base in Dayton, Ohio, and asked that certain material—including the 1955 Kelly incident file—be available for inspection.

The archive also contains an 11-page report titled "Lecture on The UFO Program," which apparently was part of an unidentified general's slide presentation for a class at the Air Technical Intelligence Center at Wright-Patterson Air Force Base sometime between 1956 and 1961.

The "Hopkinsville 'Little Green Men' Case"—discussed on Slide 42—was part of the presentation's focus on UFO cases suspected of being hoaxes.

"Many of these hoaxes are crude, others are devilishly clever," the general stated in prepared remarks for the class.

At least one Air Force officer, possibly two, visited the Kelly farmhouse to check out the stories of the witnesses who claimed to have had an encounter with space creatures on August 21, 1955, according to information contained in the Project Blue

Book file of the case. But, the military men apparently were only there in "unofficial" capacities and never took the case to higher-ups so that a full-scale investigation could be launched in a timely manner.

As a result, it was a full year later—the fall of 1956—before the new commander of Project Blue Book at Wright-Patterson Air Force Base got wind of the matter, apparently out of the blue, and through non-official channels—a memorandum from a friendly UFOlogist.

By the time the Air Force got its act together and looked into the alleged alien encounter, more than two years had elapsed since the night of terror in Kelly.

Now, the boys in blue may have been motivated to finally act, in part, because they had been tipped off that a magazine article or maybe a book was in the works and someone up there at Wright-Patterson soon would have some serious explaining to do to the public.

As a result, on August 29, 1957, Capt. Wallace W. Elwood, the assistant adjutant of the Air Technical Intelligence Center (the unit that worked Project Blue Book) at Wright-Patterson Air Force Base sent a letter to the commander of Campbell Air Force Base (at Fort Campbell), requesting any and all information on the August 1955 Kelly incident.

This particular letter is among at least 11 documents and enclosures known to be a part of the Project Blue Book case file on the Kelly Green Men.

Other documents in the file include:

❖ The memorandum, dated September 10, 1956, on the Kelly incident to the new commander of Project Blue Book, Capt. George Gregory, from J.A. Hynek, the astronomer and professor known nationwide for his UFO research.

❖ A document that appears to be a memorandum written by Capt. Gregory. Although the date is unclear, it most likely was produced sometime after the Hynek memo that advised Capt. Gregory about the Kelly UFO case. In his memo, Gregory expresses concern the Air Force, because it had not yet fully investigated the matter, was in a position to be embarrassed by the forthcoming publicity on the case. *"It is for this reason all possible information is being collected on this sighting."*

- ❖ The official reply to Capt. Elwood's letter seeking information on the Kelly case, dated October 1, 1957, from 1st Lt. Charles N. Kirk, who then was serving as the adjutant at Campbell Air Force Base.

- ❖ A letter to Lt. Kirk, dated September 17, 1957, from Capt. Robert J. Hertell, the Campbell Air Force Base adjutant at the time of the Kelly incident, informing him what he knew about the strange case.

- ❖ A statement provided to Lt. Kirk on September 26, 1957, from Maj. John E. Albert, who, in August 1955, was a reserve officer training at Campbell Air Force Base and living in Gracey, Kentucky. Albert made an unofficial visit to the Sutton-Lankford farmhouse, hours after the incident.

- ❖ A typed copy of a handwritten statement about the events at the Kelly farmhouse signed by Glennie Lankford and provided to authorities through Maj. Albert. It's unclear whether Albert wrote out the statement and Mrs. Lankford only read and signed it that morning when questioned, or whether she was the sole author of the entire document. Albert also signed the document, apparently, at the very least, as a witness.

- ❖ A copy of an unsigned and undated sketch of a "little man," apparently drawn from the descriptions provided by the farmhouse occupants. The artist is not identified nor is there any explanation about the origin of the sketch. The sketch most likely was drawn by Andrew B. "Bud" Ledwith, a Hopkinsville broadcaster who interviewed the Sutton-Lankford family only hours after the little men allegedly landed their flying saucer in Kelly.

- ❖ A copy of Joe Dorris' front-page story in the August 22, 1955, edition of the *Kentucky New Era*, reporting the UFO incident the day after it occurred.

- ❖ A copy of another Kelly Green Men story that appeared in the September 11, 1957, edition of the *Kentucky New Era*, reporting on the continued interest and notoriety of the local UFO case.
- ❖ A copy of a magazine article—with handwriting scribbled on it, which apparently contained some kind of reference to a monkey painted silver. This article supposedly came from the Sutton-Lankford farmhouse.

Of these fascinating records, the ones that stand out are Maj. Albert's official statement and the Glennie Lankford-signed copy of a handwritten account of what happened that night in Kelly.

Here is Maj. Albert's statement—presumably put down on paper more than two years after the Kelly incident and not the same morning of its occurrence—exactly as it appears in Project Blue Book (bad punctuation and bad sentence structure and all):

"On about August 22, 1955, about 8 a.m., I heard a news broadcast concerning an incident at Kelly Station, approximately six miles North of Hopkinsville. At the time I heard this news broadcast, I was at Gracey, Kentucky, on my way to Campbell Air Force Base, where I am assigned for reserve training. I called the Air Base and asked them if they had heard anything about an alleged flying saucer report. They stated that they had not and it was suggested that as long as I was close to the area, that I should determine if there was anything to this report. I immediately drove to the scene at Kelly Station and located the home belonging to a Mrs. Glennie Lankford, who is the one who first reported the incident. (A copy of Mrs. Lankford's statement is attached to this report.)

"Deputy Sheriff Batts was at the scene where this supposedly flying saucer had landed and he could not show any evidence that any object had landed in the vicinity. There was nothing to show that there was anything to prove this incident.

"Mrs. Glennie Lankford was an impoverished widow woman who had grown up in this small community just outside of Hopkinsville, with very little education. She belonged to the Holy Roller Church and the night and evening of this occurrence, had gone to a religious meeting and she indicated that the members of the congregation and her two sons and their wives and some friends of her sons, were also at this religious meeting and were worked up into a frenzy, becoming very emotionally unbalanced and that after the religious

meeting, they had discussed this article which she had heard about over the radio and had sent for from the Kingdom Publishers, Fort Worth 1, Texas and they had sent her this article with a picture which appeared to be a little man when it actually was a monkey, painted silver. This article had to be returned to Mrs. Lankford as she stated it was her property. However, a copy of the writing is attached to this statement and if it is necessary, a photograph can be obtained from the above mentioned publishers.

"It is my opinion that the report of Mrs. Lankford or her son, Elmer Sutton, was caused by one of two reasons. Either they actually did see what they thought was a little man and at the time, there was a circus in the area and a monkey might have escaped, giving the appearance of a small man. Two, being emotionally upset, and discussing the article and showing pictures of this little monkey, that appeared like a man, their imaginations ran away with them and they really did believe what they saw, which they thought was a little man.

"The home that Mrs. Lankford lived in was in a very run down condition and there were about eight people sleeping in two rooms. The window that was pointed out to be the one that she saw the small silver shining object about two and a half feet tall, that had its hands on the screen looking in, was a very low window and a small monkey could put his hands on the top of it while standing on the ground."

Maj. Albert's statement, addressing the sighting of a flying saucer at the scene, concluded: "It is felt that the report cannot be substantiated as far as any actual object appearing in the vicinity at that time."

The mention in Maj. Albert's statement of a magazine article about a silver-painted monkey is strange and interesting, and it should be noted that Yann Mege, the UFOlogist from France, apparently mentioned the very same thing in his investigation. He claimed Glennie Lankford, shortly before a meal on August 21, 1955, showed family members an article on flying saucers with a photograph of a monkey covered with silver paint.

Lt. Kirk, who most certainly one day became Capt. Kirk, but not the same "Captain Kirk" who commanded the Starship Enterprise on its voyage through the final frontier in TV and silver screen installments of *Star Trek*, marked the typed version of the original handwritten statement with Glennie Lankford's signature as a "certified true copy" at the time he forwarded the document to Project Blue Book officials at Wright-Patterson Air Force Base.

Here is that statement in its entirety (incomplete sentences, spelling errors and all) as it appears in Project Blue Book, dated, "8/22/55":

"My name is Glennie Lankford age 50 and I live at Kelly Station, Hopkinsville Route 6, Kentucky.

"On Sunday night, Aug. 21, 55 about 10:30 P.M. I was walking through the hallway which is located in the middle of my house and I looked out the back door (the word, **'south'** is inserted here) *& saw a bright silver object about two and a half feet tall appearing round. I became excited and did not look at it long enough to see if it had any eyes or move. I was about 15 or 20 feet from it. I fell backward, and then was carried into the bedroom.*

"My two sons Elmer Sutton age 25 and his wife Vera age 29, J.C. Sutton age 21 and his wife Aline age 27 and their friends Billy Taylor age 21 and his wife June, 18 were all in the house and saw this little man that looked like a monkey.

"About 3:30 A.M. I was in my bedroom and I looked out the north window and saw a small silver shining object about 2 ½ feet tall that had its hands on the screen looking in. I called for my sons and they shot at it and it left. I was about 60 feet from it at this time. I did not see it anymore.

"I have read the above statement and it is true to the best of my knowledge and belief."

As previously stated, this handwritten statement—some of its content most likely raising even more questions, including the claim Mrs. Lankford was 60 feet from the little man looking into her bedroom window—contained the apparent signatures of Glennie Lankford and Maj. Albert of the Air Force.

Capt. Hertell, who was the adjutant at Campbell Air Force Base at the time of the Kelly incident, was unable to provide any significant information about the case in the letter he wrote to Lt. Kirk.

Although he admitted to "vaguely" remembering it, and discussing it with Maj. Ziba B. Ogden, the then-deputy base commander who Hertell believes could have visited the scene in

Kelly, the captain claimed he was never directly connected with the case.

Furthermore, he noted that Col. Donald McPherson, the base commander, never ordered an official investigation into the incident, to the best of his knowledge.

"At the time, Col. McPherson figured that there wasn't anything to it, and we all followed suit so to speak," Capt. Hertell stated in his letter. *"There seemed to be nothing at all in the story that would in any way lend credence to it so we all promptly forgot it."*

Although Hertell didn't offer an opinion about what actually may have happened in Kelly, he brought up something he had heard from someone else.

"An interesting sidelight was the fact, told to me by several of the local authorities, that the farmer put up signs at the entrance to his property and was charging $1 per head 'to see where the Mars-Men landed,'" Hertell claimed in his letter, which Kirk also officially marked as a "certified true copy."

Another interesting tidbit provided by Hertell was an account of his direct involvement in another UFO case he claimed was reported and looked into several months before the Kelly incident, on a farm south of Hopkinsville. According to Hertell, a prominent attorney (identified as a "Mr. White") and one of his laborers observed *"an unidentified object streak across the sky, perform several abrupt changes of course, and finally disappear in the direction of Bowling Green, Kentucky."*

Some UFO researchers, however, disagree on the precise location of this particular UFO sighting, arguing Hertell was confused and actually may have been referring to a documented incident that occurred in Bowling Green on February 18, 1955.

Investigating UFO sightings, if anything, can be a murky science, at best.

It's never as simple as black and white.

There's always a gray...Or, as readers soon will find out ...perhaps that should be GRAYS. A bunch of them. Looking for mischief.

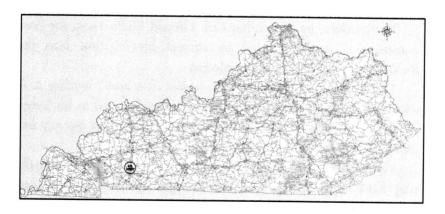

Kentucky state map (above)
Close up of the location of Kelly, Kentucky (below)

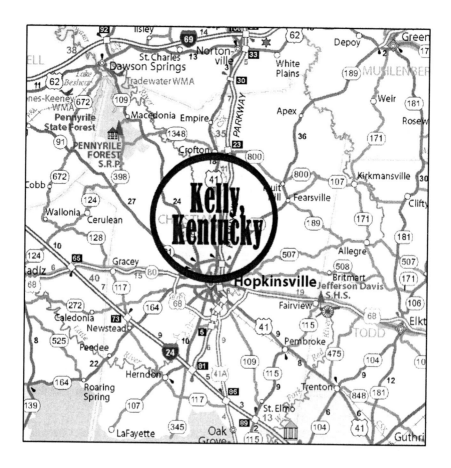

THE UFO INVESTIGATOR

If there was anyone on this Earth who knew the Kelly Green Men case inside and out—it had to be Isabel Davis of New York City.

Although this distinguished lady had *no direct knowledge* of this famous UFO case and actually lived several hundred miles away in another state, she was the driving force—with some help from a few others—behind what likely is the most comprehensive scientific study ever done on the Kelly incident.

Born in 1904, Davis was one of the country's first female UFOlogists.

As a UFO investigator, working with Ted Bloecher and Lex Mebane, she founded the Civilian Saucer Intelligence of New York in 1954. She also was the co-editor of the CSI newsletter, a respected publication that reported on UFO information.

Davis visited Hopkinsville in late June 1956, less than a year after the Sutton-Lankford clan allegedly battled the space creatures on their farm. Investigating the incident, with plans to publish her results at some point, she interviewed many of the witnesses and investigators who had played major roles in the hard-to-believe human drama.

The Center for UFO Studies (CUFOS) published her work and that of Ted Bloecher in early 1978. Davis and Bloecher's report explored the growing UFO phenomenon and was titled, *Close Encounter at Kelly and Others of 1955*. Davis undertook a field investigation of the Kelly UFO case, and her work included interviews, maps, illustrations, photographs and materials from the Air Force's Project Blue Book.

Spending at least four days in Hopkinsville, Davis was assisted in her field investigation by a Hopkinsville man, Andrew B. "Bud" Ledwith. An engineer-announcer at Radio Station WHOP, Ledwith had ventured out to the Sutton-Lankford farmhouse hours after the incident, and he drew several sketches of the little men based on descriptions provided by the eyewitnesses.

In addition to interviewing Glennie Lankford and Bud Ledwith, Davis, in her field investigation, also questioned the following people: Alene Sutton, Juanita McCord (a niece by marriage of Glennie Lankford's and the occupant of the farmhouse in June 1956); Hopkinsville Police Chief Russell Greenwell; Hopkinsville Police Sgt. Malcolm Pritchett; Deputy Sheriff George Batts; Kentucky State Trooper Russell N. Ferguson Jr.; Kentucky State Trooper G.W. Riley; Harvey Reeder, staff photographer for the *Kentucky New Era*, and his wife, Lucy; Tom Covington and Joe Dorris of the *Kentucky New Era*; and Frank Cameron of Radio Station WHOP. A telephone interview also was done with a Kentucky state trooper identified only by his last name—"Simpson."

It was not possible for Davis to interview easily the two most important eyewitnesses in the case—Lucky Sutton and Billy Ray Taylor. The men and their wives no longer were in the area during the summer of 1956.

The Suttons, native Kentuckians, presumably lived out their lives in the Bluegrass State. Not so for Billy Ray Taylor and his wife, June. They apparently never returned to Kentucky. For sure, no one ever saw them in Kelly or Hopkinsville. They just kind of slipped off the face of the Earth, never to be heard from again.

Ledwith provided Isabel Davis with a detailed, multi-page written statement of events and conversations that occurred between the hours of 11 a.m. and 10:30 p.m. on Monday, August 22, 1955—the day he, with the help of Mike Lackey, son of the owner of Radio Station WHOP, spent hours at the Kelly farmhouse, interviewing the family members and drawing sketches of the little men.

Davis noted that Ledwith *"wrote them up in the evening after his interviews."*

During a 2005 *Tennessean* interview with Tim Ghianni—one of this book's co-authors—Lackey, at the time 64 and living in South Georgia, recalled his memories of the visit to the farmhouse. *"There was no physical evidence,"* Lackey said. *"I kind of remember walking around the house with Bud. I think there was a screen that was knocked out from the shotgun fired through the window."*

According to Lackey, someone also had set up a concession stand on the property. *"I guess you could use the term, 'carnival-like atmosphere,'"* he noted.

Interestingly, on a day that would change his life forever, Ledwith had the day off from work, but went to the WHOP studios anyway around 11 a.m. for help with a problem he was having with his hobby of amateur radio. *"Everyone I saw greeted me with, 'Have you seen the Little Green Men yet?' I inquired, and got a vague account of the night's happenings."*

So, there you have it. Talk already was occurring in the community about "Little Green Men," and the alleged incident had only been reported to police 12 hours earlier the previous night.

Ledwith, in the invaluable written account he provided to Davis, stressed the seven adults at the farmhouse who had seen the little men recounted *"parallel stories"* during his interviews in two different groups and provided information that led to *"almost identical"* sketches. *"I was greatly impressed by the sincerity shown by both the men and the women. And one other fact was in evidence: When I arrived that morning the women were still badly frightened, and they had not gotten over it when I last saw them."*

Ledwith also obtained one additional piece of information that, if true, showed the government's keen interest in the Kelly case, according to Davis.

Hours after the last little man was seen, Billy Ray Taylor went hunting with a neighbor, as he had promised to do that weekend, and the two men reportedly watched as two military planes circled over the fields and woods on the Sutton-Lankford farm.

Davis, in her field investigation, targeted three principal theories suggested by skeptics in their attempt to try and explain

46

the circumstances of the Kelly incident: *The case involved mistaken identification, hallucination or imaginative delusion, or simply was a hoax.*

In her comments, the UFO investigator was particularly harsh on those people who believed the occupants of the farmhouse might have misidentified escaped monkeys from a traveling circus as little men from outer space.

Now, there was a circus in town...In fact, there apparently were two in the area the weekend of the supposed alien invasion.

Davis noted that a group of trucks belonging to the *"King Circus"* passed through Hopkinsville, heading west on U.S. 68, sometime that fateful Sunday night. The trucks reportedly stopped to exercise the camels and horses at some point between Hopkinsville and Cadiz, a considerable distance—maybe 20 miles—from Kelly and Old Madisonville Road.

Skeptics of the Little Green Men story, who supported the monkey theory, had even suggested that some of the circus trucks—containing monkeys—may have gotten lost and made a wrong turn while passing through town and then spent some time on U.S. 41 (Madisonville Road) near Kelly the night of the saucer incident.

The official 1955 schedule for the King Bros. Circus puts a few holes in the monkey theory. The circus performed in nearby Murray, Kentucky, on Friday, August 19, 1955, and the next day, Saturday, August 20, 1955, it already was in Springfield, Tennessee, for a show presumably that night.

In all likelihood, the circus wagons traveled east—not west—from Murray, along U.S. 68, into Hopkinsville and then took U.S. 41 south into Springfield. The schedule of performances also makes it quite clear that the circus had to have passed through Hopkinsville sometime late Friday night or Saturday—not Sunday, August 21, 1955, when the little men made their appearance in Kelly.

Old copies of the *Kentucky New Era* also show that the fifth annual Shrine Circus played in Hopkinsville on Thursday, Friday and Saturday, August 18-20, 1955. Admission to the nightly performances was $1.10 for adults and 60 cents for children. Some of the circus stars even went out to Western State

Hospital—known in its early days as the "Lunatic Asylum"—that Friday to perform for the patients.

Sunday, August 21, 1955, apparently was a rest or travel day for the Shrine Circus.

In any event, Davis' investigation found no evidence of any circus anywhere in the immediate area reporting that it had monkeys on the loose the night of the Kelly incident.

"But let us grant that this hypothetical sequence of events did in fact take place: Our troubles with the monkey explanation have only begun. For monkeys are hairy creatures, monkeys have long tails, monkeys are notorious chatter-boxes, and monkeys struck by bullets bleed and die," Davis wrote in *Close Encounter at Kelly and Others of 1955.*

"Yet this theory asks us to believe that seven adults, some of whom must have seen monkeys at one time or another (we recall that two of them worked for a carnival), persisted, for three hours, in mistaking hairy, long-tailed, noisy, vulnerable creatures for silvery, silent creatures with no tails, that were not injured by bullets fired at them at point-blank range. The investigators saw no more monkeys, or blood of monkeys, than they saw little men; but when they had gone, back came the monkeys, looking and behaving just as non-simian as before."

In later years, long after Davis had died, skeptics and doubters added owls and cats to the list of creatures that might have been mistaken that night for little men from outer space.

As for the theory the Kelly incident was a result of overactive imaginations or some kind of hallucination, Davis thought this theory, too, was ridiculous. The occupants of the farmhouse, throughout the investigation of the case, stuck to the same story, she noted.

"Furthermore, as the psychologists often remind us, excited people under emotional stress usually give quite different reports of the same event. But all these frightened adults saw virtually the same panic-producing objects and experienced practically the same sequence of events. If this was a shared hallucination, it was surely one of the most unanimous, consistent and durable examples on record."

The fact the Sutton-Lankford family never pursued publicity or profit as a result of their ordeal shot down the hoax theory, in Davis' opinion.

48

In light of the obvious holes in the skeptics' theories, Davis wrote in *Close Encounter at Kelly and Others of 1955* that only the *"truth"* theory holds up to scrutiny.

She added, *"In view of the nature of the story, this is not an easy assumption to make. But on the hypothesis of truth, and only on this hypothesis, no one does anything out of character: We are not required to postulate mysterious motives, secret stores of little-known information, and subtleties of purpose and temperament that are not only incongruous but ludicrous for such a family. Their behavior is consistent at every point with what else we know about their background, their individual personalities, and the situations in which they found themselves."*

Davis' affiliation with CSI lasted about 12 years. After the organization disbanded, she joined in 1966 the Washington, D.C.-based National Investigations Committee on Aerial Phenomena (NICAP). At NICAP, she held an administrative and editorial position, contributing to the NICAP bulletin—"The UFO Investigator"—and special reports.

Later in her life, she went to work for the American Psychology Association, and in 1979, helped create the Fund for UFO Research (FUFOR). She remained a member of the FUFOR executive committee until her death in June 1984.

Two years later, FUFOR created the Isabel Davis Award for outstanding contributions to the organization and UFO research.

So what were Isabel Davis' closing thoughts on the Kelly incident?

"In weighing the evidence for and against the truth of the Suttons' strange tale, there is one consideration that ought to be irrelevant. Whether or not we want the story to be true—whether or not we like the idea of "little men"—should not weight the scales one way or the other. In reality, of course, this illegitimate weight has outweighed all the others.

"Were it not for this universal determination to disbelieve a story of this nature, it is probable that the 'explanations' we have examined would never have been given serious consideration. But perhaps it is unreasonable to expect the human race, which for so many thousands of years has considered itself unique in the universe, to judge without bias a report that we might have had a visit from the neighbors."

HOLLYWOOD'S SILVER SCREEN

Since the mid- to late-1980s, the story had circulated throughout the Hopkinsville and Christian County community, and it made people smile with pride: Kelly's legendary Little Green Men heavily influenced Steven Spielberg to make his wonderful family movie, *E.T. the Extra-terrestrial.*

Rumor or truth?

The answer came—FINALLY—from the lips of the famous director himself in an interview with *Entertainment Weekly* magazine. The interview was published in the December 9, 2011, edition of the publication.

Apparently, Mr. Spielberg first learned about the Kelly incident from Dr. J. Allen Hynek, who was a technical adviser for his 1977 film, *Close Encounters of a Third Kind.*

Spielberg admitted to the magazine's loyal readers—which include the authors of this book—that *E.T.* was not even originally on his radar screen in the early 1980s.

He told the magazine he had been on track to do a film called *"Night Skies,"* which was based on the Kelly-Hopkinsville UFO incident, where a family is terrorized while fighting off little space creatures attacking their farm.

Of course, the story—and the visiting alien known as "E.T."—eventually became a lot more family friendly by the time the original script evolved into the fine film that hit the silver screen in 1982 and warmed so many hearts.

50

Hungry for additional facts, the authors of this book reached out to Mr. Spielberg for an interview, but the elusive director was nowhere to be found.

Not that it really matters. In the long run, some things probably are better left to the imagination

Over the years, the Kelly incident has received much more than just the Hollywood treatment. Books have been written about the alien encounter in Kelly, and the case has been mentioned in other publications that deal with UFO sightings.

Television, too, has taken to liking the Little Green Men case. A handful of documentaries on Kelly have played on Cable TV *(The History Channel* and *Arts & Entertainment Network)* in recent years, and Barcon Video Productions put out its own take on the bizarre tale when it released *Monsters of the UFO* in 2005.

The little men of Kelly even made it into a comic book once.

In 1997, Issue 32 of *The X-Files*, put out by Topps Comics, examined the legendary Kelly encounter. The edition carried the title, "Crop Duster."

The story centers on a modern-day resident of Kelly who reports that Little Green Men are stalking him, which brings Agent Fox Mulder and Agent Dana Scully to town to investigate.

Of course, the two agents take a close look at the 1955 Kelly incident for clues to the new mystery.

What happens?

They discover that an area factory operating back in the 1950s may have been used by a nearby military base for secret scientific experiments.

But that kind of stuff only happens in movies and comic books, right?

The truth is always out there—somewhere.

LONNIE'S STORY

After we took a left just past the old Lunatic Asylum, leaving Russellville Road for Otis Circle, I had to admit to being … well, not nervous … but anxious.

Did the man who saw the Little Green Men on August 21, 1955, really live down the road in this little working-class cluster of small homes, dogs and the occasional basketball hoop?

If so, what would he be like? Would he even talk to us?

Those were good questions. I really didn't know what I'd say, if anything, to some long-haired guy in a Hawaiian shirt who, with a tie-wearing buddy, came knocking on my door, begging me to talk about the day I saw Martians, or whatever......

Getting a little bit ahead of myself here. It's just that the Civil War-era building with the giant white columns that overlooks the section of Hoptown where we were searching for our Little Green Men witness is a pretty damned imposing structure. Now, in this politically correct time, they refer to this state mental health facility as Western State Hospital. But me, I like to call it the "Lunatic Asylum." Gotta admit, I felt quite at home when we passed that grand building on this boiling hot, mid-July day in 2005. Which is fitting, as some would say I belong there. My buddy, Rob, too. Neither of us would really have grounds to disagree.

It was down in this Hopkinsville, Kentucky, neighborhood that we would learn one of life's most important lessons: "Monkeys Don't Wear Silver Suits," which, when you think of it, really makes sense, but I'm not sure why.

Anyway, the Day of the Silver Suits began innocently enough as I arrived at City Hall to meet up with the mayor's chief administrative aide and adviser, my old newspaper pal Rob Dollar (or "Mr. Death" as he's known in the gin mills and political circles of Western Kentucky.)

When I walked into the Mayor's Office, Rob was busy talking on the telephone, handling some very important city business. An irate resident of the city was complaining about the mosquitoes at his house and the fact the city still had not been around to spray his neighborhood.

"If it's not Little Green Men, it's those damn mosquitoes," Rob joked, after spying me sitting in the office's reception area with a big grin on my face.

On this day, Rob would be driving me around—in the mayor's car, no less—to visit sites and people connected to the legendary alien invasion that had occurred a half-century earlier just north of town.

Now, this wasn't just any mayor helping me out, either. It was Rich Liebe, decorated for heroism and devotion to duty as a soldier and a police officer.

A true friend of The News Brothers who had become the respected singing mayor of Hopkinsville, Rich, a damn nice guy, was in his second term in office as a "People's Mayor" who threw all of his energy into always doing good.

Now, Rich, who I often call "Da Mayor" for no other reason than it makes me smile, didn't come up with the idea for the community to celebrate the 50th anniversary of the alien invasion at Kelly. But he certainly aided and abetted it by turning his right-hand man in the Mayor's Office, Rob, loose to help organize and coordinate the first-ever festival to promote what many believed could become a major tourist draw.

This was big. The Little Green Men Festival now was just weeks away, on track for August 18-21, and officials were looking to drum up some interest with as much publicity as humanly possible.

You can forget about your Old-Time Fiddlers' Conventions, Sorghum festivals and Harvest Days celebrations: Hoptown hoped to send its Little Green Men celebration into orbit by drawing alien fanciers and wannabe space captains from around the world. It would be kind of like Bonnaroo, the early summer celebration down in Manchester, Tennessee, but without the music, the crowd and the hippies. Probably no magic mushrooms and cactus either.

Rich and other community officials believed it would bring plenty of green into a city that was fighting hard to bolster its population and quality of life offerings so as to better compete with neighboring Clarksville, Tennessee, for the title of being "the best place for soldiers to retire and raise their families."

Sure, things were pretty good already. But Da Mayor and Rob and Chamber do-gooders and tourism bean-counters wanted to lasso the moon so they were always reaching for the sky.

"This is a 'Scuse me while I kiss the sky' type of tourist development," I later told Rob, as I did my best Jimi Hendrix impression. Of course, in Hoptown they not only were kissing the sky, they were going to infinity and beyond to draw some dollars to the historic old city.

It actually was Rob who started the ball rolling on the original idea for the festival back in his days as a reporter and editor at the *Kentucky New Era*. In August 2001, he wrote an entertaining column, arguing that the Hopkinsville community was missing a golden opportunity by not promoting its ties to a famous UFO case. He pointed to the constant stream of tourists to Area 51 in the Nevada desert and the annual festival and alien museum in Roswell, New Mexico, two other famous landing sites for spacely critters and their mother ships.

Cheryl Cook, the director of the local tourism commission, read Rob's column with great interest that fateful night while lying in bed. "It made the hair on the back of my neck stand up," Cheryl later confessed.

I don't know if she got up from bed to brush those hairs back down, but as she lay there, she began pondering the idea.

An intelligent woman, she knew a good thing when she heard about one, and, with the 50th anniversary of the Kelly incident just around the corner, there was time to get ready and make something happen. But the clock was ticking. It was put up or shut up time if Hoptown wanted to have a golden anniversary celebration for the Green Men's visit to Christian County.

While Rob is humble when it comes to claiming credit for getting the Kelly Green Men celebration launched, he certainly used his political power and his connections as a former newspaperman as well as his reputation as a damn nice guy to help the inaugural festival flourish beyond expectations.

Of course, one of his duties was to spread the word. That's where I come into the picture. The telephone rang one afternoon as I was sitting at my desk in the offices of *The Tennessean* newspaper, a then-thriving and respected morning publication next to a railroad yard just outside downtown Nashville, Tennessee.

"Flap, how would you like to see where E.T. was born?" Rob asked, knowing I was a longtime fancier of the little guy whose only wish was to go home. Years and years ago when I was young and the hero was never hung, I had visited the back-lots of Universal Studios in Hollywood, California. While at the tourist attraction, I was enjoying the sights, like visiting the shark that attacked the guys who needed a bigger boat in *Jaws*, but for some reason I kept looking over to a mysterious sound stage that was closed off from the public.

"E.T." it said on a large sign on the outside of the building. The tour guide explained that young Steven Spielberg was making a movie inside that big barn, but no one was allowed anywhere near it as he worked his magic. "It's about a spaceman or something," said the bouncy guide, who had many of the assets that could make her a starlet one day. But that's not really important here.

What is important is that Rob knew my weakness for E.T. When that movie first came out in 1982, I'll bet I saw it a half-dozen times at the theater in Clarksville, Tennessee, where I lived and worked at the time. One hot summer afternoon, the entire News Brothers entourage skipped out on work a couple of hours early to go and hide in the theater and see the film.

But that's enough about my love for E.T. Let's get back to the Little Green Men. Course, as you know by reading this book so far, they are basically the same thing.

I figured that a trip to Hopkinsville was better than spending the day inside the gloomy confines of the newspaper office, waiting to be stabbed in the back by someone from the growing army of corporate thugs who had infiltrated America's newspapers. Besides that, I did indeed want to see where E.T. was born and the idea hatched for the immortal phrase, "Little Green Men." So I talked my bosses into letting me spend a day in Hopkinsville, which is only about an hour from downtown Nashville. Yet with guys like Bird Dog roaming the streets, it does seem like another world. And that's before local officials began talking about how spacemen could come to the aid of the economy.

Other things, besides the search for the elusive Little Green Men witness, happened on the day of my visit to Hoptown. Rob presented me with a Key to the City and told me he had officially proclaimed it "Tim Ghianni Day" in Hopkinsville, Kentucky. Also, I was given what I was told was an executive pardon from Da Mayor for a traffic ticket I received just inside the city limits decades before, after going to see The Lone Ranger at the Western Kentucky State Fairgrounds. Of course, that's another story for another day. Suffice it to say The Lone Ranger, the late actor Clayton Moore, became a News Brothers friend for life. To this day, I still maintain my innocence for that terrible crime I was accused of back in January 1983. All I did was try a little bit too hard to make it back to work in time to put out the Clarksville paper when I was snagged for speeding by an unsmiling Kentucky State Trooper by the name of Rudy Adams.

All of this background is to impress on everyone that I had been given the Royal Treatment by Da Mayor and his Chief of Staff after I arrived in town to do a story on the Kelly Green Men.

Fact is, Da Mayor—who had a pretty nice city car, a green, late-model Buick LaCrosse—asked Rob to take me in that shiny vehicle to see the Green Men sights. All we had to do was drop the big guy off at a coffee shop where, I believe, he was going to meet up with some of his Green Beret chums, probably to talk over the most-recent war ....

Green Berets fittingly play a part in the Green Men saga, but we'll save that story for another time.

So Rob and I were set loose in Da Mayor's big green car, complete with police scanner and shotgun rack, so I could find enough information for a Little Green Men Festival story for Nashville's only daily newspaper. This was back when there were daily newspapers.

We visited many people on that day. And some either helped reinforce the belief in the Green Men or completely discounted the space visitors as the result of too much "alky-hall" at that farmhouse in Kelly.

All of the conversations were interesting, all right.

But the person I most wanted to spend some quality time with was Lonnie Lankford, who, as a 12-year-old boy, had been hiding under a bed at the time the firefight raged with the aliens 50 years prior to my Hoptown visit. He was one of only a few still-living witnesses who had personally experienced that night of terror.

Rob, one heck of an investigative reporter, was the fellow who tracked down Lonnie and discovered that, after all these years, he still lived in the area. Of course, he picked up the clue to Lonnie's whereabouts only after seeing him interviewed on a network cable television program. Nothing gets past ol' Rob.

"He lives around here someplace," said Rob, as he nursed the big green car down Otis Circle, with the Lunatic Asylum still in our sights.

"I've just got to see him, Death. He's the key," I muttered.

Neither of us was really a fanatic or die-hard believer in the Green Men story. But, because our disturbed minds are usually open and never closed (although occasionally "out of order"), we didn't rule it out as complete fiction, either.

So, with every interview in the city and out in Kelly that day, I became more and more intrigued, as did my chauffeur, Da Mayor's right-hand man.

As we were in search of Lonnie on Otis Circle, we saw an older guy, sucking on a Swisher Sweet, walking along the street. Rob stopped and I rolled down my window.

"Sir, do you have any idea where Lonnie Lankford lives?" I asked.

"Nah. Never heard of no Lonnie Lankford around here," the man replied.

Rob and I pressed on with our search-and-find-Lonnie mission, going further up Otis Circle and then veering off to the left until the paved street ended near a little white house and storage building. Could this be Lonnie's house? We weren't sure so we took a chance and knocked on the door. No one answered, and we didn't hear anything but some barking dogs inside the house.

Rob and I both had the proverbial "creeps" as we stood outside this house. We had no idea if we were even at the right spot or if there was someone in the house who hadn't heard our knock or simply didn't want to come to the door.

After about five minutes of waiting, we climbed back into Da Mayor's car and headed back down the road, where again we encountered the guy with the stogie, still apparently out for a slow walk in the shadow of the Lunatic Asylum.

Again, Rob slowed, and I rolled down the window.

"Sir, you sure you don't know where Lonnie Lankford lives?" I asked again.

"Never heard of him," he replied.

Then, just as we were about to drive off, the fellow held his cigar up into the air and lightly tapped his head with it. He had just experienced an epiphany. "Oh… you mean Lonnie Lankford. Why he lives just down the road. Go up this street and then take a left at the curve and stop at the little white house."

Unless I was mistaken or this was the "Twilight Zone," Lonnie Lankford lived in the exact house we'd just visited. Of course, there was another possibility: Our cigar-smoking Good Samaritan may have just escaped from the Lunatic Asylum, and didn't know Lonnie Lankford from SpongeBob SquarePants.

Rob and I decided to take our chances and make a return visit to the house.

So back we went and more boldly we pounded on the door. "Just a minute," answered a soft male voice—almost drowned out by the barking of the dogs—somewhere on the other side of the door.

The front door opened, and there in front of us, separated only by a screen door, was a man wearing a white T-shirt. He had a friendly face, a quizzical smile and a Chihuahua dog in his arms.

I introduced myself, and, in an attempt to sell myself, smiled so hard my cheeks hurt. "I really want to talk to Lonnie Lankford about the Little Green Men," I said. "Are you Lonnie Lankford?"

"Nope," replied the man, who then stood there and watched our smiles drop into frowns. Then, he laughed. "Who the heck you think I am? I'm Lonnie. I'm the guy who knows the truth about what happened in Kelly. C'mon in, fellas."

Inside, Ernest Tubb played on the stereo. "Don't make 'em like ET anymore," Lonnie said. Of course he was talking about Ernest Tubb, but I couldn't help but think of the little guy with the heartlight.

"You boys sit down. Me 'n' Cricket are just sitting here watching the television," he said, signaling me to sit down in the Easy Chair that faced his own "spot," where he sat down with the Chihuahua in his lap.

"Cricket"—Rosie Bilyeu, the love of Lonnie's life—sat across the room, nearer Rob, and she petted the bigger dog. I don't know what kind it was. But I don't think that matters. It was a big dog and it liked to bark.

The Chihuahua's name was Honey. The big dog never introduced himself, so I never got his name.

At the time of my interview, Lonnie was 62 years old. He had had a hard life, working at a variety of jobs over the years as a laborer. Although he and Cricket lived a simple life, they were computer-literate and even hooked up to the Internet.

"I don't like to tell this story too often because people make fun of me," Lonnie said. "But it really happened. Mama told me about it."

We had heard theories all day.

We had been told that Lonnie's mom, Glennie Lankford, who died in October 1977, and others in the house may have been drinking too much or they had some hallucinations that night.

Another skeptic mentioned that the circus was in town and some monkeys had escaped and that's what was mistaken for the "alien invaders." Still, others believed the family had perpetrated a hoax or that the "floating" space creatures actually were territorial owls. Someone even had the audacity to bring up a newspaper article that blamed the commotion at the farmhouse that night on a cat.

Lonnie grew somber.

"My mother never drank alky-hall," he told us, adding that it was not even allowed inside the farmhouse for anyone to drink.

He called her "a good Christian woman," who would never lie.

Which was all the reason he said he needed not to doubt that aliens visited his home in Kelly, Kentucky, on the night of August 21, 1955.

"Mama told me about it," was his don't-mess-with-me answer when I asked how he could be so sure that space creatures had terrorized the family's farmhouse. After all, hadn't his mother stashed him and his two younger siblings underneath a bed for safety?

"I don't remember much about it," Lonnie confessed.

Lonnie's sweet mother, who is said to have been a stern woman who didn't abide fools or tomfoolery, is the heart and soul of the alien invasion story.

Right up until her death, Glennie Lankford swore that she was startled when she saw an alien at her bedroom window during that long ago night of terror.

She screamed, which led to a one-sided gun battle in which two grown sons and one of their friends blasted away at the creatures.

The late Hopkinsville Police Chief Russell Greenwell, who responded to the pleas for help on that fateful evening, never really believed in the Green Men. But even so, he couldn't completely discount the story, and for the rest of his own life, whenever he recounted that strange night, he always emphasized that Glennie Lankford had "a deep fear in her eyes."

Of course, the chief may have been sympathetic because he, himself, had supposedly seen a UFO just three years earlier—along with dozens of other people—near Kentucky Lake in far Western Kentucky.

And don't think he didn't pay for it. One out-of-town reporter, who was at the Hopkinsville Police Department a few days after the alleged Kelly saucer landing, reportedly witnessed Greenwell on the receiving end of some good-natured ribbing from some of his men. One jokester asked the chief whether he had *"caught any little men lately"*...

"Aunt Glennie," as Glennie Lankford was known affectionately (despite that deep fear in her eyes) throughout the Kelly community, resisted all efforts to capitalize on the incident.

According to published reports, the family wanted nothing to do with Hollywood's interest in the alien invasion story.

Remember, from the days of Buck Rogers to Darth Vader and beyond, weird alien tales have had huge box office appeal. Now pushing on a half-century since its release in 1968, film fans still wonder what Stanley Kubrick's masterful *2001: A Space Odyssey* was all about.

It was the family's refusal to cooperate that may have led Hollywood to move the location of the movie *E.T. the Extra-terrestrial* elsewhere and turn the precisely described aliens into the lovable little guy who was marooned on Earth and is adopted by a little boy and his family. I think there's a good chance the little boy could have been patterned after Lonnie Lankford, but no one can testify to that fact.

According to Glennie Lankford's description to the media and UFO enthusiasts, the Little Green Men had big heads, round eyes and webbed feet and hands and stood around 3 feet tall. Pretty close to the image of the lovable little guy who chowed down on Reese's Pieces.

Lonnie told me that even though the legend keeps referring to the aliens as Green Men, they were never described as green in color by his mother, "They wasn't green. They wore silver. Silver suits."

Co-author Rob Dollar (right) and Lonnie Lankford, who was one
of the eleven occupants in the Kelly farmhouse the night of a
Close Encounter of the Third Kind, pose for a photograph
at the 2011 Little Green Men Days Festival in Kelly, Kentucky.

Apparently, the Green Men image was the creation of some newspaper headline writer, probably someone with an imagination who just couldn't resist the temptation to marry up the perfect color for some aliens who showed up in a town with the name of Kelly. The luck of the Irish and all, you know: Kelly Green.

Lonnie said that in a lot of ways the little guys in silver suits ruined his life. His Mama wouldn't lie, so she was made fun of. And so was he, for just believing in her. Many people also got filthy rich off the Green Men story, but not him or his family. They never made a dime.

The best way to explain what may or may not have happened in Kelly is to recall some of the things Lonnie Lankford told me during my extensive interview with him, which led to the publication of a story that appeared in *The Tennessean* newspaper on August 7, 2005.

Like all stories, but especially those recalled decades after they occurred, there are some noticeable inconsistencies with some of the facts of the case established through other witnesses.

Here are some of Lonnie's memories, as told to me, for my story in *The Tennessean*:

"*He (Lonnie) doesn't recall specific events. He was only 12 and 'Mama put me and my little brother (Charlton) and little sister (Mary) beneath a bed.'" He does remember "the commotion."*

"*I do know what Mama told me," he says, recalling the details supplied by the woman who had been widowed twice. Lonnie's pop, Oscar Lankford, a World War I veteran, died a year before the aliens attacked.*

"*A house full of people," including Lonnie's siblings, friends and cousins had just attended a revival up the hill at Kelly Holiness Church, where one of Glennie's great-nephews still pastors.*

"*We was all sittin' around eatin' supper," says Lonnie. "One of my brother's friends, Billy Ray Taylor, had to go to the bathroom. We didn't have no plumbing, so he went outside.*

"*When he came back in he said he saw something round, with lights all around that blinked" in the sky. The gathering dismissed his flying saucer report, because "Billy Ray was known as a joker."*

Eventually everyone went either home or to bed, which was where the widow was when she saw a big-eyed alien at her window.

"She sat right up in bed. Screamed. My half-brother ('Lucky' Sutton, a carnival worker who had that nickname tattooed on his fingers) had a double-barrel shotgun, so he came in there and shot through the window. According to Mama, it didn't hurt the creatures."

Glennie put the younger children beneath her bed while the older boys ran outside. "Lucky" blazing away with his shotgun. "My brother stuck his head out the door and one reached over and grabbed him by the hair," Lonnie continues. "There was several of them on the roof. He shot at them. After that we was pretty scared."

The aliens, who in various reports either floated or at least were very light on their webbed feet, were only stunned by the gunfire.

"Mama told me that a bunch of us went in the car and went to town," to get help, says Lonnie, adding that state, city and county officers as well as Fort Campbell MPs and investigators responded. "They had machine guns, rifles, pistols. All walking around and someone stepped on a cat's tail and everyone hit the dirt...."

According to Lonnie—and he has no reason to question his mom—the next day "authorities went out and seen a great big round spot in the field."

Of all the things that troubled Lonnie during our long interview on that day in the tidy little home by the Lunatic Asylum, he was most disturbed that the media and some of the good citizens of Hoptown wrote off the whole Kelly incident as the result of a family indulging in distilled spirits.

Let me pick up a little more from that interview with Lonnie that was published in the *Sunday Tennessean*:

"My brothers drank some, but my Mama never allowed it in the house. There was no alky-hall there that night.

"That's what Mama told me." That's good enough for him and he figures it ought to be good enough for anyone. His life has been plagued by ridicule because of the story "Mama tried to protect us ... She didn't talk about it much."

Despite his quiet anger at his family's treatment, he finds mirth in one published theory.

"The circus was in town and supposedly a bunch of monkeys escaped. They said these was the aliens. These simply was not monkeys. Monkeys don't wear silver suits."

When Lonnie said THAT ("Monkeys Don't Wear Silver Suits"), I looked in Rob's direction. My pal was nodding his head. "You know, Flap, that's true. I've never seen a monkey in a silver suit."

I smiled back. "In my time, I've seen a lot of evil corporate bastards in sharkskin suits, but never a monkey in a silver suit."

With that, our afternoon with Lonnie was about over. I can't remember for sure now, but I think a rerun of *My Favorite Martian* was on TV and Lonnie kept shifting his eyes from me to the TV screen. Probably he identified with the Bill Bixby character, who always seemed to be suffering from the trouble that "Uncle Martin" the alien (Ray Walston) brought into the house.

With the end of the interview, it was time to say our goodbyes and head out.

"Lonnie, thanks for all of your time," I said. "Cricket, thanks for letting us into your home. It's very nice."

Cricket made Lonnie promise Rob that he would attend at least part of the Little Green Men Festival.

"We'll come to the costume party and dance at the Convention Center, for sure," Lonnie told Rob. "Me 'n' Cricket are going to dress like aliens."

As we walked to the car, with great big smiles, Lonnie tagged along. He hugged both of us and thanked us for coming...and listening to his story without judging him.

"Lonnie, I learned a lot from you, but one lesson I'll never forget is that monkeys don't wear silver suits," I said.

"Most of them never even get dressed," Rob added.

The monkey talk got me thinking about another monkey that had been a big part of my life when I was young and the hero was never hung.

Tears welled in my eyes.

"Remember Chico?" I asked, in reference to an old newspaper story Rob and I worked on in Clarksville back in 1982 in which an escaped pet monkey got eaten by dogs. "He wasn't wearing a silver suit. If he had been, the dogs probably couldn't have ripped him into so much furry monkey meat."

Rob and I climbed back into Da Mayor's big green car. It was time to pick him up over at the Skyline Drive firehouse, where he was yelling at some firemen for sitting around too much. Da Mayor needed to get back to the office to work on some more of his crowning achievements, with Rob's help, of course. There were keys to the city to be presented, water parks to build, citizens to calm, mosquitoes to kill, trash to be picked up ... not to mention the sometimes contentious City Council meetings, which Da Mayor almost always asked Rob to attend to keep track of shenanigans.

As for me, it was time to head back to Nashville, or as I always call it "going back down the hill," because the drive to Music City in the Cumberland River Valley seems to be a long, gradual descent. But before I began that drive, I knew I was going to make a quick stop at a convenience market

I was craving some Reese's Pieces.

First, of course, we needed to get Da Mayor back to City Hall, where my car was parked and waiting for me.

As Rob and I rode away from Lonnie's house, the same strange man we'd encountered two hours before was still standing by the roadside, his cigar long extinguished, looking up at the Lunatic Asylum.

Then, things really got weird. I lost myself for a moment in a daydream. Rob was having the same bad dream, too...I think.

As I eyeballed the man with the fascination for the Lunatic Asylum, he now appeared to be holding a small sign that I think had the date *"AUGUST 21, 2017"* written on it.

In my state of apparent delusion, Rob and I looked at each other, not knowing what to make of the cryptic message we both thought we were seeing.

The Lunatic Asylum, for some reason, made me think about the great psychologist Sigmund Freud.

"You know, Mr. Death, Sigmund Freud was deathly afraid of the number 62," I said to myself, not even realizing the words were coming out of my mouth since I think I was in some kind of trance.

Rob, who was lost in the same trance, turned white as a ghost. "Flap…August 21, 2017, is 62 years to the day that the little men visited Kelly. This is crazy. But, maybe they're coming back…"

When the car hit a pothole in the street, the loud thump apparently brought us back to reality. Rob and I rubbed our eyes and looked back in the direction of the strange man. He was smiling, but there was no mysterious sign in his hands.

The man then waved at us, and we waved back. It was then that I really took time to notice how short he was and how his hat barely fit on his oversized head.

The sun glinted off his worn, silver suit.

'EARTHLIGHTS'

Remember when E.T. turned on his heartlight in that great movie that got its inspiration from the reports of little space men terrorizing the Sutton-Lankford family at their farmhouse in Kelly, Kentucky?

As an aside, do you also remember Neil Diamond—with songwriters Carol Bayer Sager and Burt Bacharach—penning that truly sappy top-of-the-charts song that played off *E.T. the Extra-terrestrial* back in 1982?

It was called *"Heartlight"* and became one of Mr. Diamond's signature songs.

The story behind the song is kind of heart-warming. It seems the three songwriters saw the Steven Spielberg film together and were so moved, it led them to write their hit song.

When E.T. leaves Earth in the movie, if you recall, his heart glows a luminous red. Hence, the title of the song.

The authors wanted to ask Mr. Diamond a few more questions about *"Heartlight"* and maybe even sing a few verses with him. But, he's a busy guy—you know, singing his sweet songs for Boston Red Sox fans as well as continuing to be one of pop music's most powerful and popular voices—and never got back to us.

Now for the rest of this feel-good story. Ironically, in the end, there was a price the trio had to pay for feeling so good and creative. The songwriters reportedly were required by a court to write Universal Studios a check for $25,000 for the use of ideas from the film.

OK. Enough about the heartlight...There's no evidence at all that any little men with heartlights floated around the fields of Kelly, Kentucky, in late August 1955. And, as far as the authors can tell, the Kelly Green Men case had no heroic little boy who saved a friendly alien, riding off into a moon-lit sky with the creature on the handlebars of his bicycle. Maybe our pal, Lonnie Lankford, could have filled that role. But, of course, the aliens that invaded Kelly apparently weren't friendly and bicycles couldn't fly back in the 1950s.

Let's go in another direction. You ever heard of "earthlights"?

When I first got involved in studying the Kelly incident—after my good friend, Rob Dollar, pretty much spearheaded Hopkinsville's celebration of the 50th anniversary of the rather unusual events—I spent a fair amount of time exploring the strange Kelly tale for a package of stories I did for the August 7, 2005, editions of *The Tennessean* newspaper.

Rob, at the time, was doing his job of trying to drum up interest in the festival. As noted, he was the top lieutenant to hard-working Hopkinsville Mayor Rich Liebe, a guy so tough in his previous careers as a soldier and a lawman that he makes the late McNairy County, Tennessee, Sheriff Buford "Walking Tall" Pusser seem like a sensitive, new-age guy. No, Liebe never clubbed gangsters with a big stick, but he was a no-nonsense kind of lawman, a sort of Western Kentucky version of Wyatt Earp.

I still marvel all these years later that Rob and the Hopkinsville-Christian County Convention & Visitor's Bureau and Da Mayor (my name for Rich, a most-blessed fellow) could dream up and organize an out-of-this-world celebration of a legendary event that supposedly took place several miles north of the city limits. Course they pulled it off in high style.

I went up to Hopkinsville and to the scene of the infamous alien invasion to report on the Kelly legend. I have to acknowledge that I'm something of a believer in aliens. How else can you explain the popularity of soccer as a spectator sport?

Anyway, on a late summer day back in 2005, I walked Old Madisonville Road and the yard near where the farmhouse once stood and the gun battle took place. I discussed it with the county historian—my new friend, old "William T."

Now, this observer of history let me know he's always been of the "alky-hall did it" School of UFO Debunkers. *"My opinion is that they'd been dippin' into what we in the local vernacular call 'Panther Juice,'"* he told me as we stood within sight of the middle of "downtown" Kelly.

Much of what appeared in that series of dispatches from those days in late August 1955 appears elsewhere in this book, as Rob and I are trying to be as complete as possible in our investigation.

We have presented theories of monkeys and territorial owls and, of course, plain old intoxication as the reasons for the occurrence or the reports of those strange events. Of course, the truth—what the farmhouse occupants said happened actually happened—could have been another explanation.

Back to my visit to Kelly.

Joining me and Rob and Mr. Turner on that highway on that hot, July morning was Gail Cook, who lived for a short time in the house attacked by the aliens after Glennie Lankford packed up her family and high-tailed it for the big city lights of Hopkinsville.

"I remember there was a big, burnt-spot out there where nothin' could grow," she said in the interview, conducted on the main highway, U.S. 41/Madisonville Road, and then on Old Madisonville Road, which runs beside the property where the aliens fought her family.

She also shook off all of the skeptics and doubters, claiming that she had experienced a similar UFO occurrence back in 1997, when she was operating a restaurant in downtown Kelly.

"About 25 of us actually seen it," she told me. "It was in August, too. Not sure if it was the exact date or not. It was muggy like this, though. There was this ship that come flying over. My sister lived upstairs in an apartment over the restaurant. She called and said there was a spaceship. I said 'Oh it ain't!' but I got over there.

"It was like a dusty dawn. We saw these lights. It was there for about 2½ hours. We sat and watched this ship.... It would come up, and the frogs and crickets would get quiet."

Gail told us the *"round with a bunch of lights"*-spacecraft let at least one passenger get out. In her mind, there was no coincidence that a creature in a black veil was seen standing by the road the next morning before he/she/it magically vanished.

We'll get other accounts later, but I always found Cook's tale—which she told me while holding out her right arm to illustrate the position of all the activity—interesting.

Now, law enforcement authorities had no reports or records of the Cook incident in their case files. Apparently, newsmen living in the area at the time (like co-author Rob Dollar, who was working for the *Kentucky New Era* newspaper in 1997) just flat out missed the Story of the Century.

Of course there are debunkers galore, and they get their time and just treatment in this book.

I suppose some of you probably are wondering what I meant when I earlier brought up the subject of "earthlights."

When I got back to Nashville, where I worked at the time at the daily newspaper, I decided to explore various theories that might explain the Kelly incident.

Among the most fascinating came from Greg Little, a Memphis, Tennessee-based psychologist whose specialty is criminal treatment, but who also studied alien encounters in his work.

He had previously visited the Kelly site, known throughout the world as the location of *"one of the most-documented UFO incidents"* in history.

Little claimed the folks who blamed "Panther Juice" or white lightning were dead wrong, as drunks don't hallucinate. (He never interviewed me and Rob about this, for the record.)

But he also dismissed the idea that aliens could have been responsible for the commotion that night.

"I don't think there has been any sort of extraterrestrial visitation at all," he told me back then in my interview. Instead, Little said he was not alone among his colleagues in the space-invasion field who believed the sighting was caused by how *"electro-magnetic fields interact with human brain chemistry."*

He said such electro-magnetic fields are associated with geologically active areas and pointed out that the New Madrid

Fault—an earthquake disaster waiting to happen as it cuts across a piece of the Midwest and Mid-South—passes not far from Kelly.

Little explained that "earthlights" caused by the electro-magnetic fields escape into the air.

"It's a charged ball of plasma," he told me for my *Tennessean* story. *"It glows, rotates, like any magnetic field would do if suspended in the air."*

When Billy Ray Taylor saw what he believed was a rotating spacecraft outside the farmhouse in Kelly, what he actually was seeing likely was a rotating earthlight, according to Little.

Little theorized that, as the plasma got closer to the farmhouse occupied by the Sutton-Lankford family members, the electro-magnetic fields triggered a reaction with their brain chemistry.

"They began to perceive it was something else," he told me.

The Kelly legend about space creatures invading a farm and battling the occupants—what Little maintains were figments of electro-magnetic-field-infected brains—not only inspired the movie, *E.T. the Extra-terrestrial,* but also played a big role in a popular Mel Gibson flick. *"The creatures in Signs are based in part on the Kelly-Hopkinsville fairies,"* Little said.

Looking back on my interview with this interesting psychologist, I still have a bone to pick with him. Personally, I took offense with him using the term *"fairies"* when talking about the Kelly space creatures.

I've always believed that everyone—even a space alien—is entitled to his or her own lifestyle choice.

The Kelly Church Road sign marks the intersection with Old Madisonville Road. About 300 yards up the road is the farmland in Kelly, Kentucky, where the aliens "attacked."

WHEN 'CLOSE' COUNTS

Whether you believe in flying saucers—some people call them Unidentified Flying Objects (UFOs)—or not, there is a good chance you have experienced a Close Encounter of Some Kind.

The J. Allen Hynek Center for UFO Studies (CUFOS) actually has scales to measure the Close Encounters with alien spacecraft. They were established by the late Dr. Hynek himself.

"Close," by the way, means within 200 yards, the length of two football fields.

Most people have learned of Close Encounters mainly from the Steven Spielberg movie about the Third Kind of such an occurrence, and we'll get back to that shortly.

Because both authors have heard many tales of such occurrences, we consulted Dr. Mark Rodeghier, scientific director at CUFOS, to determine the basic definitions of Close Encounters.

Many Internet sources list more classifications, but you know the Internet: Anybody can post something, and there are those who presume it to be true.

The good doctor replied to our request for clarification most likely because of the confusing Internet reports, and he responded quite clearly.

"There are six different types of report classifications, but only three types of Close Encounters," he said.

"Later, others added Close Encounters of the Fourth Kind, which refer to abduction reports, but that wasn't approved by Dr.

Hynek (although he might have done so had he lived long enough)."

So, first of all, let's go with the actual Close Encounters... the two-football-fields-away-or-less sightings or interactions with spacemen or at least spacecraft.

Dr. Rodeghier gave us permission to use the actual CUFOS definitions and information from the organization's official Web Page.

So, here we go:

Close Encounters of the First Kind (CE-I): *Though the witness observes a UFO nearby, there appears to be no interaction with either the witness or the environment."* **(CUFOS)**

In the Kelly incident, this first kind of encounter began on the big night. Billy Ray Taylor, one of the people in the Sutton-Lankford farmhouse that night, had either gone out to use the outhouse (as our friend Lonnie Lankford told us in our 2005 interview, based on the story told to him by his mother, Glennie Lankford) or he was just going to get a bucket of water from the well (the more-common report). In any case, he saw something that startled him. *"When he came back in he said he saw something round, with lights all around that blinked,"* Lonnie explained. No one believed Billy Ray Taylor at that time.

Now, no one, and the authors mean no one, has gone through life without seeing "something" out there. But most don't accept it as alien life and say it was a Close Encounter of No Kind At All.

Some folks write these off as the proverbial "swamp gas" sightings. Others say people who think they saw a spaceship that close are simply quite mad. The authors respectfully disagree, as we believe in just about everything, including the basic goodness of humankind. Although, we also know that during our years of living in and around the Fort Campbell Army Post—near Hopkinsville, Kentucky, and Clarksville, Tennessee—the strange visions in the night sky could well have been some sort of stealth aircraft used by our favorite secretive helicopter unit.

Who knows? Uncle Sam may have equipped Seal Team Six and "The Night Stalkers " of the 160th Special Operations Aviation Regiment (Airborne)—the highly-trained and cut-throat stealth units responsible for terminating Osama Bin Laden and for many other unreported but presidentially-mandated killings—with some virtually otherworldly craft and equipment.

Close Encounters of the Second Kind (CE-II): *These encounters include details of interaction between the UFO and the environment which may vary from interference with car ignition systems and electronic gear to imprints or burns on the ground and physical effects on plants, animals and humans.* **(CUFOS)**

Had the Kelly eyewitnesses never come face-to-face with the monkeys in silver suits, the owls, the cats ... or the aliens ... there still would have been a record of this type of Close Encounter. The day after the big shootout with the Martians or whomever, the area lawmen went out to the field where Billy Ray Taylor saw the object while taking a leak or getting water.

"Authorities went out and seen a great big, round spot in the field," Lonnie claimed in our interview, of this apparent burn-mark left by the space landing or maybe the space takeoff.

His cousin, Gail Cook, told the authors in a separate interview the very same day, that *"there was a big, burnt spot out there where nothin' would grow."* Ever.

Of course skeptics have their explanations and they may be right. Still, this obviously was a Close Encounter of the Second Kind.

Finally, the big one:

Close Encounters of The Third Kind (CE-III): *In this category, occupants of a UFO—entities that are humanlike ("humanoid") or not humanlike in appearance—have been reported. There is usually no direct contact or communication with the witness. However, in recent years, reports of incidents involving very close contact—even detainment of witnesses—have increased.* **(CUFOS)**

This, of course, was the basic occurrence in the Spielberg movie of the same name. In fact, most encounter-with-aliens movies from Hollywood are of this Third Kind. Remember, E.T. hid out among the stuffed animals in the kids' closet. Definitely a Third Kind of Encounter.

And who can doubt that the Kelly incident qualifies, what with all the shotguns-blasting, hair-pulling, yelling and general ruckus of the extended firefight and its reprise after the lawmen—who had come out to investigate—had gone back to Hoptown.

In an effort to be as comprehensive as possible, we should go on to mention that there is another type of encounter which is not close at all. These are called Relatively Distant Sightings by CUFOS.

Here are the definitions, thanks to the good scientists of that organization:

Nocturnal Lights: *These are sightings of well-defined lights in the night sky whose appearance and/or motion are not explainable in terms of conventional light sources. The lights appear most often as red, blue, orange or white. They form the largest group of UFO reports.* **(CUFOS)**

While you may well dispute that the sights were caused by aliens, there is no chance any readers have not experienced some sort of unexplained Nocturnal Lights during their lifetimes. Baby Boomers, including the older of the two authors, may have written these sightings off to tripping or bad mushrooms.

Daylight Discs: *Daytime sightings are generally of oval or disc-shaped, metallic-appearing objects. They can appear high in the sky or close to the ground, and they are often reported to hover. They can seem to disappear with astonishing speed.* **(CUFOS)**

In short, these could be spacecraft, experimental flying war-craft of some sort or a really, really bad case of swamp gas.

Radar-Visual Cases: *Of special significance are unidentified "blips" on radar screens that coincide with and confirm simultaneously visual sightings by the same or other witnesses. These cases are infrequently reported.* **(CUFOS)**

While not regularly reported, it was during the Cold War that all of us who were alive were made aware of these blips, which usually were said to be signs that the Commies had aircraft in the vicinity. That's why folks started building bomb-shelters and stocking them with crackers, evaporated milk and cans of baked beans.

Heck, it would not be unlikely that at nearby Fort Campbell—where a top-secret facility known as "The Birdcage" once operated—some sorts of aircraft were ascending into the sky, causing blips, discs, nocturnal lights and more back in 1955 ... and maybe even today for that matter.

But then again, these really could be spacemen and their souped-up, field-burning vehicles. We'll leave that up to you. At least up until 2017.

THE 50-YEAR ANNIVERSARY

"Will THEY Be Back?"

Short, sweet and to the point. And, of course, so very mysterious.

It was this four-word question that would become the catchy slogan and theme for the Hopkinsville-Christian County community's first-ever celebration of the legendary Little Green Men of Kelly.

Cheryl Cook, who headed the Convention & Visitor's Bureau, had always liked the idea of a festival centered on the Kelly alien encounter, particularly since reading my *Kentucky New Era* column in the summer of 2001 that had urged city fathers to seize the opportunity.

Realizing the 50th anniversary of the Kelly incident was just around the corner, she immediately saw gold and not silver, since the silver anniversary had long since passed with barely a notice. The idea for a Little Green Men Festival had been safely squirreled away for the proverbial rainy day in the not-too-distant future.

In the Spring of 2004, the time had finally come to start planning the big celebration. But first, local officials had to determine if there was any public support for a Little Green Men Festival.

On Thursday, May 20th, sometime after the noon hour, the tourism director began e-mailing some interesting people in the community who loved Little Green Men or, at the very least, had vivid imaginations.

One of those e-mails popped up on my computer. I guess Cheryl Cook figured that Rob Dollar, the former newspaperman who only a few months earlier had started his new job as the executive assistant to Hopkinsville Mayor Rich Liebe, was someone who always dreamed BIG and surely could sell the town on celebrating LITTLE Green Men.

Another e-mail popped up on the computer of Tim Golden, a former radio and television newsman who now was in the mental health business as the public information officer for the multi-county, Hopkinsville-based Pennyroyal Center.

Cheryl's e-mail began: *"We need your help on this fun project for Hopkinsville and Christian County. You've been recommended to attend a "Brainstorming Session" for a very fun event for Hopkinsville-Christian County in August 2005. This does not obligate you to serve on any committee or do any work. We just need people who can think outside of the box for one hour.*

"...Let your imagination run wild. Come to the Commerce Center, 2800 Ft. Campbell Boulevard, Thursday, May 27 at 5:00 P.M. Who knows you may want to be a part of this exciting event! But even if you don't, we will certainly benefit from your imagination at the 'Brainstorming Session.'"

Now, if Cheryl Cook's return address had not been on the e-mail, recipients might have let their imaginations run wild with thoughts from the dark side....Who wants to pick my brain for one hour? The Little Green Men? And just what do they mean by "pick?"

The big day to brainstorm about a Little Green Men Festival arrived with little fanfare and about 15 to 20 people showed up at the Commerce Center. Some people will tell you the attendance was just about right for the number of people in Hopkinsville who possess the ability to THINK...outside the box, of course.

Many of the happy faces belonged to Little Green Men believers, while others at the meeting were just the usual do-gooders and true believers in capitalism-at-any-cost...You know the crowd I'm talking about..."The Beautiful People" who are always looking for new ways to make more and more green so they're able to continue to throw their weight around town and get their way.

The meeting generally focused on potential activities for a Little Green Men Festival. Participants—some still honing their skills at thinking outside the box—mentioned such possibilities as a parade, dance, costume contest, yard sale, UFO exhibits and vendors, an arts and crafts fair, and even scientific programs and lectures.

The mayor's right-hand man—ME—suggested a forum or roundtable at the fairly new, multimillion-dollar Hopkinsville-Christian County Conference & Convention Center, where eyewitnesses and others with direct knowledge of the Kelly incident would join UFO experts in what would be the first-ever public discussion of the legendary flying saucer case.

As an aside, a few years later, there was a campaign to rename the convention center for a retiring state representative, Jim Bruce, who was first elected to office in the early 1960s and served longer than any other lawmaker in the history of the Kentucky legislature.

Wanting to honor their Hopkinsville friend, Bruce's colleagues in the state legislature promised to send a $1 million grant our way to retire the convention center's debt—but only if the building was renamed for Jim Bruce.

Wouldn't you know it? The facility is now called the James E. Bruce Convention Center, and that, my friends is a lesson on how public buildings sometimes are named in Kentucky.

Now back to the idea for a Kelly Green Men forum.

Tim Golden volunteered to videotape the event so the first-person accounts could forever be preserved for history. There was even some talk the project might generate some money through DVD sales.

Remember the interesting woman who told Flap that amazing UFO story when they met in Kelly? Well, we heard it first. She was at our meeting and told the very same story to the brainstormers, many of whom lacked vivid imaginations. The Little Green Men already had returned to the area, at least once, just seven years earlier, and their hovering UFO was seen by a restaurant full of people, she claimed.

Everyone in the room grinned or nervously smiled. Yep. We were getting into the proper spirit to pull off one doozy of a celebration, all right.

So inspired and moved by the idea of celebrating one of America's most famous UFO cases, Ron Sydnor, an African-American and former Marine, actually penned a poem about the little men of Kelly and their flying saucer.

An excited Cheryl Cook e-mailed me a copy of the one-page poem—titled, "The Kelly Incident"—the day after the meeting.

It inspired me, too.

Here is the ending verse: *"...But, for those who saw it, we called them insane, Because, what they saw we could not explain, So, if you are ever on the Kelly scene, Keep your eyes peeled for the 'Kelly Green Men.'"*

When he wrote his poem, Sydnor was employed by a Chamber-related organization. Years later, he would become the park manager of the Jefferson Davis State Historic Site in Fairview. I'm not sure if he ever wrote a poem about Jefferson Davis, but if he didn't, I think he should consider it.

Sydnor's poem was never used by the Little Green Men Festival's publicity machine. I don't remember the reason. Maybe it got lost in all the excitement.

Now, let's return to the story about the birth of the festival.

After the conclusion of Cheryl Cook's brainstorming session, not much happened for about a year. Like all committees that start out with good intentions, the members took the snap, but handed off the ball to make things happen to a small group of doers who would actually plan and coordinate the festival

The elite Little Green Men Team consisted of a persistent bunch of folks with the ability to talk the talk and walk the walk: Cheryl Cook, Betsy Gore Bond of The Chamber, George McCouch of the *Kentucky New Era*, Tim Golden, and me.

Like all good things, the work got done, and Hopkinsville soon was publicizing its Little Green Men Festival, a four-day celebration of activities that would run from Thursday, August 18, 2005, through Sunday, August 21, 2005.

The media were pestered weeks and months ahead for pre-festival publicity.

My old pal, "Flapjacks" Ghianni, responded with a masterpiece in the *Sunday Tennessean* that put the spotlight on Lonnie Lankford, one of the few witnesses still alive who was in the Kelly farmhouse when the aliens landed their saucer back in August 1955.

A college buddy, Don McNay, author of a weekly newspaper column syndicated across the country, helped out by making fun of then-Kentucky Gov. Ernie Fletcher for his job performance and ME for helping organize a festival to honor Little Green Men.

Even my old newspaper, the *Kentucky New Era*, got into the act, producing a 16-page special section—"It Came From Kelly," printed on no less than GREEN newsprint—that greeted out-of-towners and festival-goers the very week of the big event.

Back in those days, the newspaper could do projects of this magnitude because they had more reporters on the payroll and the staff itself was dedicated to serving the community on which it reported. Nowadays the only kind of green paper newspaper executives focus on has faces of presidents on it.

As the mayor's right-hand man and the official representative of the City of Hopkinsville, it was part of my responsibility to take care of the VIPs who showed up in town for what we hoped would be the festival of festivals.

At least three "dignitaries" were coming to Hoptown to participate in the festival as speakers on the UFO phenomenon: Peter Davenport, director of the National UFO Reporting Center in Seattle, Washington; George Fawcett, a UFO lecturer and researcher from North Carolina; and Dr. Joe Nickell, of Lexington, Kentucky, a paranormal investigator, author, and "Investigative Files" writer for *Skeptical Inquirer* science magazine.

If my memory serves me correctly, invitations to Steven Spielberg and William Shatner ("Captain Kirk") failed to produce any return mail. Nice try, but no cigar. Spielberg, of course, was someplace making movie magic, but it would have been great to hear from him. Shatner apparently was too busy shilling for an on-line hotel-booking outfit and generally cashing in as a caricature of his screen image.

Nevertheless, the three VIPS who did come to town were thrilled to participate in our historic festival, particularly after I gave them a dose of The Royal Treatment—a "goodie" bag full of gifts, and the Key to the City.

Now, Nickell was quite a colorful character. He was also a magician and former private eye. For his business cards, he passed out wooden nickels, and he wasn't shy about giving them out. I still have mine.

On Friday, the day before their presentations at the Conference & Convention Center, I became Davenport's and Nickell's best friend by chauffeuring them on a tour of Hopkinsville and area historical sights.

Riding around in Da Mayor's big green car, with me at the wheel, we drove up to Kelly to look at the invasion site, where the Sutton-Lankford family supposedly battled the space creatures. The old farmhouse is long gone, apparently destroyed by fire, but the well is still there. We also made stops in Hopkinsville at Edgar Cayce's grave in Riverside Cemetery and then toured the Pennyroyal Area Museum on East Ninth Street to study the Kelly Green Men exhibit and a display on Robert Penn Warren.

After experiencing some "local cuisine" during lunch at The Homestead Restaurant on North Drive, Davenport and Nickell—upon learning that the house where Pulitzer Prize-winning author and the nation's first poet laureate, Robert Penn Warren, grew up was just down the road a bit—convinced me to drive them to Guthrie.

So off we went, down U.S. 41-South, with Davenport (the UFO believer) and Nickell (the skeptic) arguing about case after case the entire 25 miles to Guthrie.

On the way, I made the mistake of telling the VIPs about the Bell Witch legend, a tale of the supernatural that involved a bad spirit or demon that spooked and tormented a family near Adams, Tennessee, during the 1800s. President Andrew Jackson, a Tennessean, even had a rather bad encounter with old "Kate" once when he was traveling through the area.

Of course, my guests were intrigued by the story and then delighted to find out Adams was very near Guthrie. So after touring the birthplace of Robert Penn Warren, we were off to Adams after getting some directions to the Bell Witch Cave from Guthrie Mayor Scott Marshall.

I know what you're thinking…No, Mayor Marshall did not give Davenport and Nickell a Key to the City. After all, they weren't celebrating a flying saucer festival in that Todd County city and didn't need to butter up any UFO experts.

Anyway, when we finally got to the Bell Witch Cave, we discovered it was not possible to walk to the entrance since it was real muddy and too far away, and the only way to get to it was to drive down an unpaved road that was more of a rocky trail.

Davenport and Nickell were looking forward to checking out the cave and challenging the spooks, but I told them there was no way I was going to drive Da Mayor's big green car down that muddy trail. I might have been wet behind the ears, but I sure didn't want Da Mayor yelling at me like he yelled at the firemen.

So, off we drove on our return trip to Hopkinsville. I think I managed to appease my badly-disappointed VIPs by taking a detour and showing them the Jefferson Davis Monument in Fairview. But the believer and the skeptic still argued all the way back to the City of Hopkinsville, "The Pearl of the Pennyrile."

Sometime later, while the festival was in full swing, I drove Nickell back to Kelly, so he could experience an old-fashioned tent revival at the Kelly Holiness Church—the same church that some of the Sutton-Lankford clan supposedly had attended only hours before their night of terror in August 1955.

The revival apparently was being held in response to the Little Green Men Festival, and many of those who attended wore T-shirts that read, "Son of Man is Coming Back."

Nickell and I spoke briefly with the church's pastor, Wendell "Birdie" McCord, who actually was related to Glennie Lankford. He was her great-nephew.

"I don't know if the green men is coming back, but I know the Son of Man is coming back," McCord told Nickell, in between the singing and his preaching.

About a year after his visit to Hopkinsville and Kelly, Nickell wrote a piece for *Skeptical Inquirer* science magazine. Based on his on-the-scene investigation, Nickell insisted the Kelly space creatures were actually Great Horned Owls.

Remember the French UFOlogist—Renaud Leclet—reached the same conclusion back in the summer of 2001, except he believed the creatures were Eagle Owls.

"C'est la vie."

When the curtain finally fell on Hoptown's most unusual festival, community leaders agreed it had been an overwhelming success.

Ever the optimist, I had predicted Hoptown—"The Center of the Universe"—would likely be visited by tens of thousands of visitors from around the world.

Alas, we came up very short of my crowd estimate. But, a good time definitely was had by all. By both believers and non-believers

If you were among those who managed to miss out on the inaugural Little Green Men Festival back in August 2005, here is what the official Schedule of Events looked like:

Thursday, August 18

❖ *Plan 9 from Outer Space, the classic science-fiction movie, 6 p.m., Hopkinsville Community College.*

Friday, August 19

❖ *"Alien Abductions" Fund-raiser, 10 a.m. to 2 p.m., Pennyroyal Area Museum.*

❖ *Exhibits on the Kelly Incident, All Day, Conference & Convention Center.*

❖ *Kids Alien Costume Contest, 6:30 p.m., Conference & Convention Center.*

❖ *Intergalactic Trade Show, 5 p.m. to 7 p.m., Conference & Convention Center.*

❖ *"What is Amateur Astronomy in the 21st Century?" (Dr. John McCubbin), 8 p.m, Conference & Convention Center*

❖ *Stargazing, 9 p.m., Outside the Conference & Convention Center*

Saturday, August 20

❖ *Exhibits on the Kelly Incident, All Day, Conference & Convention Center.*

❖ *Intergalactic Trade Show, 9 a.m. to 4 p.m., Conference & Convention Center.*

- ❖ *"What Really Happened in Kelly?" (Panel Discussion), 9 a.m. to noon, Conference & Convention Center.*
- ❖ *Symposium Programs, Dr. Joe Nickell, paranormal investigator (noon); George Fawcett, UFO lecturer and investigator (1:30 p.m.); and Peter Davenport, executive director of the National UFO Reporting Center (2:30 p.m.), Conference & Convention Center.*
- ❖ *Monsters of the UFO, (Television Documentary on the Kelly Incident), 4 p.m., Conference & Convention Center*
- ❖ *"Picnic With The Pops," (Owensboro Symphony Orchestra), 7:30 p.m., University Heights Academy.*
- ❖ *"Space Jam" Alien Ball, 9 p.m. to 1 a.m., Conference & Convention Center.*

Sunday, August 21
- ❖ *Exhibits on the Kelly Incident, All Day, Conference & Convention Center.*
- ❖ *Intergalactic Trade Show, noon to 4 p.m., Conference & Convention Center.*
- ❖ *Karaoke Contest, 1 p.m., Conference & Convention Center.*
- ❖ *Storytelling Bus Tours to Kelly, 12:30 p.m., Pick-Up at Conference & Convention Center.*

For the readers who must know, Lonnie Lankford, Cricket and a bunch of their friends showed up in full force at the Space Jam-Alien Ball.

They weren't shouting, "May the Force Be with You," but Lonnie definitely dressed for the occasion, wearing the costume of a scary-looking alien.

A few weeks after the festival, I drove to Lonnie's small white house near the Lunatic Asylum to present him with a nice plaque with a certificate that expressed the City of Hopkinsville's appreciation for his participation in our celebration.

Now a celebrity in town, Lonnie smiled.

And what about the little men? Did they return to Christian County on August 21, 2005—exactly 50 years later?

Probably not. But, if they did, I guess no one saw them this time.

Or maybe….just maybe, no one recognized them dancing the night away at the Space Jam-Alien Ball.

A video of the history-making panel discussion from the first festival devoted to the Kelly incident is still a popular item for alien enthusiasts. As some of the participants in the actual Kelly incident since have died, the DVD provides the last record of the recollections from that night.

PRESERVING HISTORY

Almost 50 years to the day when it happened—or maybe didn't happen ... well, something happened —a diverse panel of citizens with knowledge of the Kelly incident gathered together at a public forum to debate the existence of little men from outer space.

It was the first time many of these people had met each other, let alone joined together for what turned out to be a scholarly, yet impassioned, and sometimes even eerie gathering.

If this event did anything at all, it allowed spectators to leave with as many questions or maybe even more than when they came into the forum.

If they were non-believers, they perhaps left wondering how so many people could accept without question the idea of gray, no-necked creatures from outer space. If they were believers, they may have left with some doubts cast by the image of folks indulging in too much "Panther Juice" or scratched their heads over a shotgun blast that left a tiny geometrically perfect hole in a window screen.

It was Saturday, August 20, 2005, the big-draw day for the inaugural Little Green Men Festival, and a crowd of about 200 had claimed their seats at the Conference & Convention Center in Hopkinsville, Kentucky, so that they could see for themselves history in the making.

The panel discussion, with longtime Hopkinsville radio personality Hal King (who also happens to be a neighbor of Rob's) serving as the moderator, was videotaped—courtesy of

Tim Golden, a former radio and television newsman—in order to forever preserve the participants' historic testimonials.

This would be the first ... and sadly, because of age and death ... the only time this panel of witnesses to history ever would be in the same place at the same time.

The 11 panelists, as might be expected, had different versions of the truth to tell on this day. In introducing them, golden-throated radioman King declared, "To say they are in disagreement on many things is an understatement...But we are here to inform and perhaps to entertain."

At the time of the 2005 forum, there were just three living eyewitnesses who had been among the 11 occupants of the Kelly farmhouse when it supposedly was attacked on the night of August 21, 1955, by perhaps as many as 12 to15 silver-suited little men from a flying saucer.

All three—Lonnie Lankford, Charlton Lankford, and Mary Lankford—were young children of 12, 10, and 7, at the time, and hid underneath a bed while their family shot it out with the space invaders. Their mom, Glennie Lankford, had stashed them there out of fear they might get hurt in the gun-battle with the aliens.

Only Lonnie Lankford, a Hopkinsville resident and the oldest of the siblings, was at the forum.

Charlton, Lonnie's baby brother, also had been invited to tell his story at the panel discussion. But he turned the invitation down cold. Did he remember the little men in silver suits? What were his recollections of the gun battle with the space aliens? Everyone wanted to know, but Lonnie—the gentle family spokesman—informed the audience his little brother simply didn't like to talk about the incident.

Little sister, Mary, was too young at the time of the gun battle with the aliens to even remember the incident, according to Lonnie Lankford.

While Lonnie was the sole eyewitness on hand for the discussion, the family honor also was defended by true believer Geraldine Sutton Stith, daughter of the late Elmer "Lucky" Sutton.

Lucky—with brother J.C. Sutton, and Billy Ray Taylor—fought off the little men on that hot August night long ago. Their vivid descriptions of the strange lights, gremlin-like creatures, and the terror had provided ammunition for books and Hollywood films over the years... and, sadly, for snickers from non-believers and undeserved family humiliation.

Lonnie Lankford, admitting he was not very good with words, sheepishly stood up at the forum, with microphone in hand, to read a statement he had written for the occasion.

"I didn't get to see the aliens myself," he said. "But I do remember all the commotion, and I will never forget the terror that filled our home that night."

Lonnie Lankford said that for most of his life he had kept quiet about his infamous claim to fame, and it only was in recent years that he had decided to speak out about it after being contacted by the media for interviews. About five weeks before the forum, he had whiled away a good part of a Hopkinsville afternoon, detailing the events as he understood them, to the authors of this book.

In his comments at the historic forum, Lonnie also downplayed past media reports that described the night as an epic hours-long gun battle involving hundreds of shots. Remember, according to some accounts, there was a battle, followed by a break in which the family sought help from the police in Hopkinsville, followed by another fierce battle when everyone got back to the farmhouse in Kelly.

Probably six or seven shots were fired over a period of about an hour, according to Lonnie Lankford, who also insisted he had no memory of a second visit by the aliens later that night.

"There wasn't no battle," said Lonnie, a gentle and genuine soul. He was not arguing with anyone, but rather stating fact, not fiction, as he had lived it and heard it while beneath the bed.

The Hopkinsville resident also made it quite clear to the crowd that he had no doubt the visitors that night were not of this Earth.

"It's up to you whether you choose to believe or not," said this quiet and unassuming fellow.

Geraldine Sutton Stith, who was born about six years after the supposed alien invasion, recalled first learning about the incident when she was 7 or 8 after two people showed up at her home to interview her father about it.

"It was something that was kept quiet my whole childhood," she said.

In the late 1960s, Lucky Sutton took the family out to the old Sutton-Lankford farm in Kelly and showed them a "big round spot" where nothing was growing and told them that it was where the saucer had landed some 13 years before, she noted.

"Whatever happened that night, it scared him," Geraldine Sutton Stith said. "You could see the fear in his eyes. He would turn white as a ghost."

The stories she heard from her dad about the lights in the sky and the alien invasion remain with her. "A light in the sky terrifies me," she said.

No one who was with her father, Lucky, that night ever got over it, although they sure tried, according to Geraldine.

"They went to church, tried to live life right. What happened that night struck fear."

R.N. Ferguson, a retired Kentucky State trooper, who was among the first lawmen to arrive at the scene of the alleged invasion, recalled getting the telephone call about the incident.

"I did not relish being called, at night, in bed, not feeling well in the first place, and told by a state police dispatcher to go to Kelly…that a spaceship had landed," Ferguson said.

The straight-shooting lawman would have been inclined to ignore such foolishness and roll over to finish his shut-eye, if the dispatcher had not convinced him that it was no practical joke.

"…When you receive a call, you've got to go. You've got to go see…separate fact from fiction. And that's something that's been rather hard for humanity to do since the beginning of time…," the retired lawman noted.

Ferguson said he responded to the call and rushed out to the Kelly farmhouse, where he soon was joined by a dozen or more law enforcement personnel from a variety of agencies.

"When we left that night, no one had anything tangible that they could call evidence or something that had been disturbed that was not there before," Ferguson said.

Ferguson said he performed his duties that night in a thorough and professional manner. "...I examined the area. I went into the house. I talked to the people. I did everything we were supposed to do, and I found nothing," he said.

Well...almost nothing.

Apparently, there was something found that night that suggested someone may have used a tobacco stick or some other object to make a hole in a screen in an attempt to fake a bullet hole, according to the beloved lawman often referred to by moderator Hal King at the forum as "Trooper" or "Fergie."

"I didn't find anything except for one thing. I found a 1-inch square hole in a screen where they were supposed to have shot through the screen outside at something...A 1-inch square hole...I've never been able to find the weapon that (makes) a 1-inch square hole—then nor now. I've never seen one," Ferguson declared.

Ferguson has always maintained that alcohol most likely had something to do with the Kelly incident, noting that the behavior of some of those at the scene led him to that conclusion.

Challenged on the drinking theory by the moderator, Hal King, who claimed his research had revealed that lawmen found no evidence of alcohol at the scene, Ferguson quipped, "I don't know who you were talking to, but I wasn't talking to the same folks."

At the time of the forum, Ferguson was the only investigator of the Kelly case still alive.

Ferguson told the audience he had been interviewed many times, since August 1955, by people from all over the world—in person or over the telephone.

He mentioned that only the day before, a man from Oregon called him to inquire about the Kelly Green Men case.

"He told me his mother was an alien, and he's a hybrid. You figure that out."

As for the alleged barren spot on the old Sutton-Lankford farm, Ferguson said, "I've flown over it hundreds of times. I've been a passenger in airplanes that have flown over it several times...

"I've never seen anything any different except the grass grows green in the summertime and it dies in the winter."

Ferguson admitted he gets tired of talking about the Kelly incident, but it's one of those cases destined to go on forever.

"It's a question of 'I say' and somebody else says something else. I can't prove that there wasn't anything there other than the fact there was no evidence left," he explained.

"Maybe there was something there for somebody else. So, the mystery stays there when I can't prove it and they can't prove it. It just sits there. It's just back and forth and it will be that way I would imagine as long as there's anybody that wants to pursue the Kelly Green Men."

Jennifer P. Brown, a longtime reporter and editor with the *Kentucky New Era* newspaper, told the forum audience about the various stories she had done over the years on the Kelly Green Men.

She had the privilege of doing the retirement story on Joe Dorris when the legendary journalist finally put down his pad and pencil in the 1990s after more than 60 years in the newspaper business. And, of course, Joe's memories as the reporter who wrote the very first story on the Kelly incident were a big part of that assignment.

Up until his death in November 1999, people were still contacting Dorris about the Kelly incident.

"Even after all those years, he just sort of scratched his head that the story just went on and on. People could never get enough of it," Brown said.

Although the late David Riley, another *Kentucky New Era* editor, interviewed Joe Dorris on the Kelly incident in the mid-1980s and walked away with the definite impression he was very skeptical about the story of the little men, Brown claimed she just could not remember whether the veteran scribe had ever voiced an opinion around her.

When King asked Brown whether she wanted to offer her opinion on whether little men visited Kelly back in August 1955, she answered with a one-word response, 'No!" which drew loud laugher from the audience.

Brown, in her comments, also told the crowd about a 2003 story she wrote from an interview with Arthur "Hoss" Cansler, who was the police chief in Crofton, Kentucky—north of Kelly, just several miles up U.S. 41—on the night of the supposed alien invasion.

According to Brown, Cansler, now deceased, told her he believed he had actually been the first lawman on the scene, arriving at the farmhouse prior to the family fleeing to Hopkinsville for help.

"Mr. Cansler had his own theory about what happened," Brown noted. "He didn't believe the story of an alien invasion. He believed that someone that night was using a cat to sort of torment folks in the house...throwing a cat through the air...throwing a cat and having it sort of cling to a screen door...And that was his version of what might have happened."

But could that tormented cat have cut a perfect 1-inch square in the screen? Of course not....However, the abuser of the cat, if there was one, could have committed that deed, as well, as part of the night's entertainment.

Another incident recounted by Brown might have been considered a "smoking gun" in regard to the Kelly Green Men story.

Brown said she once interviewed Raymond McCord, a nephew of Glennie Lankford, while researching a Kelly Green Men story.

McCord revealed to her in 1995 that his cousin, Lucky Sutton, had confessed to him about the Kelly incident.

"Mr. McCord told me that, years after the incident, Lucky Sutton had told him in private, 'You know there wasn't anything to that,'" Brown said.

"I really don't know what to make of that...I think it's possible that Lucky Sutton could have told people that just to sort of end the conversation," she said, suggesting that perhaps he was fabricating this tale of the invasion having been fabricated, if you will, as a way to put all of the sniping and giggling to rest.

"The family has felt for years that they've been ridiculed for this...Maybe that was Lucky's way of just sort of ending a conversation."

At the time of the Kelly incident, Russell Greenwell was the chief of the Hopkinsville Police Department.

The chief's widow, Rachel Greenwell, appeared at the forum to recount her late husband's role in the affair.

She said she actually went to the farmhouse in Kelly that night with her husband, hoping to see something.

Fact is, she even drove the car to get the chief to the scene.

"I didn't see anything...But there was something in the air that made you feel like something had happened," Mrs. Greenwell said. (In an earlier interview co-author Tim Ghianni did with her for a story in *The Tennessean*, she said, *"There was an eerie sort of atmosphere around the place."*)

At the historic forum, she added: "It made you stop and wonder what's going to happen? What did happen?"

The events made for fodder at Hoptown mealtime conversations for quite some time.

The talk about the Kelly mystery "went on in our house like everybody else's house," she said of those discussions.

Rachel Greenwell also acknowledged at the forum that her husband had reported seeing a UFO near Kentucky Lake, west of the Hopkinsville and Kelly area, back in 1952.

Frank Dudas, a retired Hopkinsville Police Department sergeant, was part of the police force in August 1955, but was not working the night of the Kelly incident.

Based on his police contacts, though, he said the Sutton-Lankford family had been frightened by something.

"I think the story is possible," he told the audience. "They seen something, somebody dressed in silver."

Dudas admitted his opinion no doubt was influenced by the fact he and another police officer, Owen Chilton, had their own UFO experience in Hopkinsville just months before the little men showed up in Kelly.

Dudas said he and Chilton were on patrol on the late shift when they saw something at a high altitude in the sky that definitely was not conventional aircraft of the time. "I saw three objects. It was daybreak and I could see them clearly," Dudas noted.

Hopkinsville and Christian County's official historian, William T. Turner, mentioned the notoriety of the Kelly Green Men case in the World of UFOlogy.

"In the world of UFOs, this historian's observation is the Kelly Green Men incident is a big event in that body of knowledge," he proclaimed.

Did Turner believe Kelly had been visited by little men from outer space? The historian offered no opinion at the forum on the truthfulness of the story given by the farmhouse occupants. "In their minds, it was so," he said.

Others who were part of the roundtable discussion that day were ordinary citizens who got caught up in the excitement.

Leo Wilson, who worked for Radio Station WHOP at the time, recalled the news coverage and interviews in the days after the incident. He recounted other strange or unique occurrences and people that made Christian County famous, or infamous, so, he asked: "Why not the Little Green Men over in Kelly?"

Linda Renshaw, a former mayoral assistant, was 16 years old and lived in Kelly near the Sutton-Lankford farm on August 21, 1955. She remembered the influx of curious visitors to Kelly in the days after the incident.

Renshaw said the farmhouse occupants lived a simple life, and she did not believe they were influenced by movies, magazines or television to invent the story of the invading aliens.

"Daddy didn't believe a word of it. Of course, he didn't believe in Edgar Cayce either," Renshaw quipped. "I believe they saw something. I believe they believe what happened."

Skip Aldridge, who worked his entire life in the Circulation Department of the *Kentucky New Era* newspaper, was 14 years old and a freshman at Hopkinsville High School when he heard about the flying saucer landing in Kelly on the morning radio news. William T. Turner, at the time a teen-ager himself, was one of Aldridge's classmates and running buddies.

"It was truly the talk of the town with most of us kids," Aldridge said. "Some of them still believed in Santa Claus and The Easter Bunny."

"When this came out, we just knew it was the real thing...Aliens landing near Hoptown, a gun battle...That's as good as it gets...If I live to be 150, I will still remember how excited and everything that we all got over it."

Philip Mullins, a Hopkinsville businessman, was another teen-ager who got caught up in the moment.

Mullins said he and his father, curious like everyone else, went out to the Sutton-Lankford farm the day after the incident.

He said there were people everywhere, and he was very surprised that the police had not cordoned off the scene to protect any evidence.

"If there was any evidence there, it was probably gone, with people going just anywhere they wanted to go anytime they wanted to go," Mullins said.

In walking through the house, Mullins said he saw nothing to indicate that "these people were followers of science fiction or anything of that nature."

Mullins told the audience he saw no damage to the outside of the house from bullets or shotgun shells.

At one point, Mullins and his father actually talked to Lucky Sutton and listened to his story. Mullins said he was surprised to see the man in a farmer's coat.

"The reason I was surprised is it was 95 degrees outside, and he had this coat on," Mullins noted.

Yes, it was hot. Boy was it hot.

Mullins said he believed what Lucky Sutton and the others told lawmen.

"My evidence was in talking to that man and looking him in the eyes, and there's no doubt in my mind that there were aliens there that day," Mullins said. "I have no reason not to believe him."

Furthermore, Mullins reminded the audience that all seven occupants of the farmhouse who actually saw the little men told the same story—even providing the same unusual description, for that time in UFO sightings, of gray aliens with no necks.

"You've got to admit it's pretty hard to get seven people to sit down and say the same thing when they're not sitting in the same room together," Mullins noted.

Originally, three other people related to the farmhouse occupants—Lucky Sutton's son, Elmer Sutton Jr., and cousins Gail Cook and Norma Malone—had been scheduled to be a part of the forum. But they failed to show up for the event.

At the forum, which lasted about two hours, the audience was allowed to ask questions of the panelists, and several took full advantage of the opportunity.

Fittingly, it was Geraldine Sutton Stith, who got the last word at the forum.

She asked everyone in the audience to put themselves in the shoes of her father and others at the farmhouse, who had that strange and close encounter on the night of August 21, 1955.

Lucky's daughter defended the behavior of family members, claiming it was normal to be in an excited and agitated state under the circumstances.

"If something's coming up to my house that I can't explain, that is floating over the ground, that is silver in color, that I've never seen before....Heck yeah, I'm not going to be calm about it," Geraldine Sutton Stith said.

She continued: "It happened. It scared them. It frightened them for the rest of their lives...I know everybody has their opinion... Fine... But, you've got to look at this with an open mind. My father was terrified the rest of his life. For people to think that they were supposed to stand back and be calm about this and not be frightened is idiotic. It's just crazy...Think what you want. Believe what you want. But SOMETHING happened that night."

In the immediate years after the forum, at least three panelists, all senior citizens who had lived long and good lives, passed away—Frank Dudas, Rachel Greenwell, and Leo Wilson.

They're gone now, and others will surely follow in the coming years.

But, rest assured, no one who was at this historic forum and told their story will take any secrets to the grave.

Their memories of the Kelly Green Men case will live on— forever.

Co-author Tim Ghianni (right) interviews Brandon Seats, a distant relative of Lucky Sutton, during the 2013 Little Green Men Days Festival in Kelly, Kentucky.

Chapter 11

THE SKEPTICS

Skeptics and non-believers, in trying to make sense out of the Kelly incident over the past several decades, have pointed to just about every possible explanation under the sun.

Maybe the occupants of the farmhouse who claimed they saw little men from outer space on August 21, 1955, were drinking to the point of being three sheets to the wind.

Maybe the supposed alien invasion was simply a hoax for profit or publicity, or even a prank played on the Sutton-Lankford clan for laughs.

Maybe there was some kind of mysterious electro-magnetic field in Kelly that caused the family members to hallucinate that night, and their imaginations just simply ran hog wild.

Maybe those angry little men that everyone thought they saw were actually escaped monkeys from a traveling circus or territorial owls protecting their young, or even a cat (or cats) clawing at the window screens.

For argument's sake, let's look at the elephant in the room.

Maybe the truth was told, and little men from outer space actually landed their flying saucer in Christian County and paid a visit to the home of some God-fearing farm folks.

It begs a question, doesn't it?

"Why on Earth…Kelly, Kentucky?"

R.N. Ferguson, one of the first lawmen to arrive at the scene of the legendary battle between space creatures and the farmhouse occupants, probably posed that very question to hundreds and hundreds of reporters who traveled from everywhere to interview him over the years.

The retired Kentucky state trooper most certainly will be known forever as THE leading skeptic in the Kelly Green Men case.

His question, for sure, is interesting, and goes directly to the heart of his reasoning on the matter: If YOU were an alien from somewhere out in the galaxy, some extraordinary form of intelligent life, and you possessed all kinds of advanced technology and a spacecraft that could carry you anywhere in the Universe. Why pick Earth, and if you did, why on Earth would you land near a farmhouse in Kelly, Kentucky? Why not choose Washington, D.C., or New York City, or even London, England? Why would you visit with a farm family and not go and try to communicate with scientists or offer your hand (or claw) in friendship to the president of the United States?

Ferguson even notes that the aliens wouldn't have had to venture very far—just minutes as the spaceship flies—to find world-class musical entertainment 65 or so miles away down U.S. 41-South.

"Hell, they could have gone to Nashville," he told book co-author Tim Ghianni for a story previewing the 50th anniversary celebration that ran in the August 7, 2005, editions of *The Tennessean* newspaper. *"They certainly would have seen more."* Perhaps could have caught the Louvin Brothers, Roy Acuff, and Flatt & Scruggs, for example, at the Grand Ole Opry.

Isabel Davis, the UFO investigator, had a ready answer.

"This is hardly a weighty argument, but the question is a natural one," she wrote in *Close Encounter at Kelly and Others of 1955.*

"Extraterrestrial visitors may be just as ignorant about our lives and psychology as we are about theirs. To say, 'They should not have called on the Suttons, therefore they did not call on the Suttons' is a naïve, almost comical extension of human notions of protocol. If extraterrestrial visitors must conform to our ideas of correct behavior before we accept their existence, it is likely to be a long time till that happens."

Now, going back in the other direction, if the incident did occur as the occupants of the farmhouse reported it, then maybe the space creatures deliberately landed their flying saucer in the rural Kentucky countryside.

What could have been the reason? Could it have been Kelly's close proximity to Fort Campbell? Back in the 1950s and 1960s, Fort Campbell housed many super-secrets, most of which only became known in recent years.

The Army occupied most of the sprawling military reservation. But, there also was an Air Force Base there in 1955, and even a small Naval detachment at Clarksville Base, a 5,000-acre, high-security compound in the rear of the post that was guarded by stern-faced Marines with shoot-to-kill orders.

Don't forget, on the night of the Kelly incident, a state trooper near the Shady Oaks restaurant north of Hopkinsville reported hearing and seeing several meteor-like objects streaking across the sky. The objects, sounding like artillery shells, reportedly were headed toward Kelly from the direction of Fort Campbell and the top-secret site at Clarksville Base where nuclear weapons—including hydrogen bombs—were being stored by the government. At the time, no one other than the military and those who worked there knew what was in the storage facilities, of course.

Clarksville Base was the second of thirteen nuclear weapons storage sites established during the Cold War. Known officially as the Clarksville Modification Center, local residents called it "The Birdcage."

The facility, which included a well-sealed tunnel system carved into the side of a hill, opened in 1948. The nuclear operation shut down in 1965, with the facility then annexed four years later by Fort Campbell. The Army uses the site today as a munitions and equipment storage area.

Maybe the little men of Kelly were really interested in the nuclear secrets at Fort Campbell and the Sutton-Lankford farmhouse was only a detour.

Another legendary UFO case involves very similar circumstances.

Roswell, New Mexico, where a UFO containing extraterrestrial life supposedly crashed in July 1947, is only about 110 miles away from a location in the New Mexico desert where the United States, two years earlier, detonated its first nuclear bomb.

We would be remiss if we didn't mention another Steven Spielberg connection here. If you remember, the fourth installment of the Indiana Jones adventure series—*Indiana Jones and the Kingdom of the Crystal Skull*—begins in Hangar 51 at a U.S. military base in the Nevada desert. Without going into a lot of detail, the big action sequences toward the beginning of the film involve a scuffle between Dr. Jones and some evil Russians over the Roswell remains. It was a Spielberg movie, of course. Director Spielberg and creator and pal George Lucas, who hit it big with the *Star Wars* series, seem to have an insatiable appetite for the mysteries of outer space.

Now, let's return to those reports of meteor-like objects roaring across the sky sometime during that night of terror at the Kelly farmhouse.

Skeptics argue they could have been meteors or aircraft and not connected, at all, to the alleged invasion of little men at the Kelly farmhouse.

Jim Fleming, a longtime Christian County magistrate who grew up in Kelly, never believed in the alien invasion, although he did believe the family saw something that scared them. He told co-author Tim Ghianni his theory for the 50th anniversary story in *The Tennessean*:

"There's been so many sightings through the astronauts, airline pilots and on and on, I believe there's a possibility of people seeing different objects flying around.

"We're sending objects out into space all the time."

Remember that Frenchman? Not Renaud Leclet, the guy with the Eagle Owl Theory, but Yann Mege, the UFOlogist who visited Hoptown in April 2000.

Mege claims fireworks were set off sometime on the night of August 21, 1955, as part of a circus performance.

The fireworks may have been what the state trooper and other possible witnesses saw in the night sky near Kelly, he said.

It makes sense, but our visitor from France appears to have his facts wrong.

The Shrine Circus, indeed, was in Hopkinsville that weekend, and one of its headline acts, according to old copies of the *Kentucky New Era*, was "The Great Fussner" and his famous Spiral Tower, which often included a fireworks display.

The only problem, however, is there was no circus performance on the night the Sutton-Lankford family fought the little men. The circus had performed shows on Thursday, Friday and Saturday (August 18-20, 1955). Presumably, Sunday was a rest or travel day and there were no fireworks shot into the night sky.

Mege is among the many skeptics who firmly believe the Kelly incident must have been a hoax or some kind of prank pulled by one of the farmhouse occupants or someone else known to the family.

That explanation likely was, at least, the initial impression of Jacqueline Sanders, a contributor for *The Saucerian Review*. The 99-page booklet—published by Gray Barker of Clarksburg, West Virginia, in early 1956—reviewed flying saucer activity that occurred during the 12 months of 1955.

Sanders showed up at the Hopkinsville Police Department within days of the Kelly incident and wrote an on-the-scene story that appeared in print several months later. Her report—"Panic in Kentucky"—apparently was reprinted in *UFO Universe* magazine decades later in 1994.

According to her published report, Sanders said she was unable to interview the three principle eyewitnesses in the case—Glennie Lankford, Lucky Sutton and Billy Ray Taylor because they disappeared within 48 hours of the supposed alien invasion.

The vanishing act apparently made many people, previously sympathetic to the family, suspicious that they were behind a hoax or prank.

"Their disappearance could have been due to a number of reasons," Sanders wrote in her story on the case. *"For one thing, people came from miles around to the farmhouse, trampled over the ground, took pictures of the house, inside and out, and collected souvenirs.*

"Someone suggested the situation might be alleviated by posting a '50-cents admission' sign. But the people still came and they made it a dollar. Before

they were through, they had the price of taking pictures of the family up to $10.

"Some people may jump to the conclusion that this was the whole idea of the thing, and that perhaps the family had only made up the story. Chief Greenwell didn't think so, however. Especially since they had moved out so soon, while people were still visiting the farm."

It probably should be noted here that even modern-day skeptics know the possibility of profit exists in the Kelly tale. Tim Golden, genuine nice guy who produced the video of the historic panel discussion at the first Little Green Men Festival back in 2005, has no question that it is all a fantasy. Yet, he also doesn't mind it if people purchase one of his videos. Capitalism's boundaries go far beyond the final frontier.

Isabel Davis, the UFO investigator and co-author of *Close Encounter at Kelly and Others of 1955*, was successful in getting an interview with Glennie Lankford in the summer of 1956. Therefore, she managed to shed some more light on the carnival atmosphere around the Kelly farmhouse and the family's disappearing act.

"...following the publicity came the sightseers. The Suttons, having spent one night, according to their story, in fighting off inquisitive little men from outer space, were now destined to spend days and nights fighting off even more inquisitive human beings. Though they showed no signs of realizing it, a second and worse invasion was rolling toward the farm, and they would have no more success in getting rid of these unwanted visitors than of the first group. As the news spread, the crowds grew thicker. Their cars jammed the Old Madisonville Road. They stared and pointed. They stopped their cars, got out, walked around the house, opened the doors and walked in, asked questions, told the family to pose for pictures, laughed and made jokes. The little men had been terrifying, but at least they had stayed outside the house and had taken themselves off by daybreak..."

Davis noted that some of the Sutton-Lankford clan, sick of the unwelcome publicity and sightseers, left town within days for Michigan, where Glennie Lankford's married daughter lived. However, not long into the trip, they changed their mind and returned to Kelly because they were fearful that souvenir-hunters would trash their farmhouse, and they wanted to protect their belongings.

Sightseers continue to disturb the peace to this day. David Brasher, who back in 2005 lived in the since-demolished Spanky's Game Room in "downtown" Kelly, told the authors, when Tim Ghianni was doing his piece for *The Tennessean*, that there may have been meteors in the sky that fateful night in 1955, but that's about it.

"I don't believe in UFOs, I don't believe in space monsters. I do believe there's probably intelligence out there. But they did not come to Kelly," said Brasher, who identified himself as Gail Cook's brother-in-law. Gail, you'll recall, is Lonnie Lankford's cousin.

Although Brasher doesn't believe there was any sort of Close Encounter in Kelly, he's still amused by the numbers of folks who do. And he let us know during our visit that there had never been a shortage of strangers shy about coming to seek him out for information.

The believers continued to come and knock on his door a half-century after the fact (whatever the fact is). *"I've had people here from England. I've had people here from France,"* Brasher said. *"I don't know how they find out about somethin' like this all the way over there. I get eight or 10 a year who just come up here and knock on the door."*

Brasher isn't among those who have capitalized on the Little Green Men legend, though. He said he turned down offers of money to allow people to camp on his property. *"Why take their money when they can camp anywhere around here for free?"* he asked, looking out over the corn and soybean fields and the gently forested landscape.

The Kelly businessman also, for free, occasionally escorted the foreign visitors to the site of the gunfight, just several hundred yards away. The old farmhouse is long gone and replaced by a dandy double-wide home owned by Dorris McCord, Gail Cook's brother. Of course, as mentioned earlier, the only original fixture on that property is the well.

It should be pointed out that a few years after our visit with Brasher at Spanky's—site of past extraterrestrial mischief by veiled visitors, flashing spaceships in the night and the eeriness of a summer evening when the crickets and frogs turned silent—the business shut down. It was replaced by a pre-fabricated building that is a center for a church. Kelly may not have many people, but it sure has plenty of places to worship.

Even as traces of the original sites have virtually disappeared, the occasional visit by a UFO enthusiast is to be expected. But they aren't going to find too many folks with personal knowledge, unless they happen to go back to Hopkinsville and seek out Lonnie Lankford.

The fuss back in 1955 chased the farmhouse dwellers from their home. Several weeks after the commotion finally died down, the Sutton-Lankford family left their Kelly farm, never to return. Glennie Lankford and her three children moved into an apartment complex in Hopkinsville, and J.C. Sutton and wife, Alene, found their own place, also in Hopkinsville.

Lucky Sutton and Billy Ray Taylor, with their wives, already had returned to their jobs with the traveling carnival.

Although the "family-played-a-hoax" theory apparently is quite popular with most skeptics of the Kelly incident, there also are quite a few believers in the explanation that creatures of this Earth were mistaken for the little men.

The theory of territorial owls—advocated by skeptics like Leclet and Dr. Joe Nickell—to explain what happened at Kelly is interesting, to say the least.

Leclet, in his published work of August 2001, insisted that his theory satisfied many of the facts of the Kelly case, including the 3-foot size and strange behavior of the little men.

"Generally, an eagle owl is waiting in a tree. It flies silently, be it flapping or gliding. When the Suttons saw the eagle owl for the first time, it was perhaps swooping down on a prey, opening its wings for landing...Moreover, when an owl is excited, its ear tufts stand up vertically. They could be the big pointed ears seen by the witnesses," Leclet wrote.

"Why would an eagle owl...have been so interested in the Suttons' house? These raptors hunt rats, mice, field mice, birds, rabbits and hedgehogs, and lots of these animals can be found near a farm. The eagle owl can also attack human beings if they go too near a nest...It is precisely from August to September-October that eagle owls nourish their young...It is then easy to

understand why the creatures came again and again around the farm: their instinct led them to protect their young and to defend a territory that ensures plenty of food."

Nickell claimed in an article published in *Skeptical Inquirer* science magazine—the November/December 2006 edition—that the descriptions of the little men were very similar to the appearance of a Great Horned Owl, and that those same owls had been mistaken for space creatures in other UFO cases.

"In summary, allowing for the heightened expectations prompted by the earlier 'flying-saucer' sighting, and for the effects of excitement and nighttime viewing, it seems likely that the famous 1955 Kelly incident is easily explained by a meteor and a pair of territorial owls," Nickell noted.

With that conclusion, Nickell took one final parting shot at the legend of the Kelly Green Men: *"What a hoot!"*

Now, if the little men weren't owls, then maybe they were monkeys that had escaped from the Shrine Circus that played in Hopkinsville that weekend, or from the King Bros. Circus that supposedly passed through town.

If you remember, Isabel Davis shot down this theory pretty good, reminding everyone that the epic gun battle that night failed to produce any monkey parts or monkey blood.

Apparently, there could only be one unlikely explanation for the lack of monkey and/or owl corpses at the Kelly farmhouse: The Sutton brothers and Billy Ray Taylor, although country boys who had hunted all their lives, were just lousy shots.

Ferguson's opinion on the Kelly incident has never wavered over the years, and he never was shy about sharing it, when asked.

He likes to call himself "The Voice of Authenticity" when folks like *The History Channel, A & E* and the authors of this book come calling.

"I still haven't seen that danged spaceship," he said, with a laugh, when asked for the story by Tim Ghianni in the August 7, 2005, editions of *The Tennessean* newspaper.

The lawman jokes about that telephone call that lifted him from his sickbed and sent him out to the farm property in Kelly to look for little men from outer space.

A veteran of a career of investigations, Ferguson points to the lack of any proof of an invasion of any sort.

"You get a call to a shooting, and you find a weapon, cartridges that have been expended, even a body," said the former trooper in that *Tennessean* interview.

Ferguson, a good-hearted, good-humored man, loads his voice with flavors of skepticism and sarcasm when he talks about the missing evidence and why the space invasion perhaps has more to do with fear and imagination and less to do with reality.

"Oh, it did happen. It is a part of history. It is just what happened that is being arbitrated."

Remember, that's the same basic sentiment expressed over and over by nice guy and historian William T. Turner, who maintains he is not a believer in the slightest, personally.

But, the historian told Tim Ghianni in that *Tennessean* story, he does not disregard the vehemence of the family in asserting that aliens squared off with the folks in the farmhouse.

He said that if the family is convinced *"they experienced it, then it is so. Who am I to say it wasn't so?"*

So even the most-knowledgeable of naysayers leaves a little room for some sort of occurrence out there that night.

Course, Mr. Turner is the one who first tossed out the term "Panther Juice"—distilled spirits—when talking about what he believed really was at the heart of the occurrence on Old Madisonville Road.

Veteran lawman Ferguson echoes those sentiments.

He believed from Day 1 that alcohol had something—probably everything—to do with the report of the Little Green Men. He based his opinion, in part, on the behavior that night of some of the farmhouse occupants.

One of the turning points for him likely was the discovery of a perfectly square hole in a screen door at the farmhouse that supposedly was the result of a shotgun blast aimed at the little men. Lawmen at the scene suspected right away that a tobacco stick—for this was the heart of tobacco-growing country back when the golden leaf stood for big bucks rather than lung disease—poked through the screen made the hole, or maybe someone with a razor blade.

As for alcohol, it is true that no law enforcement officer at the scene ever reported finding any physical evidence that suggested that anyone had been drinking.

But, *Close Encounter at Kelly and Others of 1955* contains at least one interesting tidbit on this particular subject.

It was information provided to Isabel Davis by Bud Ledwith, as a result of his visit to the Kelly farmhouse just hours after the appearance of the little men.

One short sentence…Maybe a fact that got lost in Davis' lengthy report.

"Mr. Ledwith noticed a few beer cans in a rubbish basket the next day…"

Tim Ghianni (left) and Rob Dollar look over the replica of the flying saucer that may have landed near a farmhouse in Kelly, Kentucky, in August 1955. The inspection took place during the 2013 Little Green Men Days Festival.

GREEN BERETS, 'GREEN ACRES' & GREEN MEN

The better part of a century passed into history before the good people of Kelly came to the realization that a local legend was more of an opportunity and not a reason to suffer through an eternity of embarrassment.

Not surprisingly, it took a few outsiders to size up the situation and launch a campaign to embrace the Kelly Green Men.

One driving force was a retired Green Beret master sergeant by the name of Brown who moved to Kelly in 1996, while he still was in the Army. "We looked all around Fort Campbell for a place like where I grew up ... on Lake Seminole, hunting and fishing and chasing alligators." He wasn't looking for alligators in Kentucky. At that point he wasn't looking for Little Green Men, either. He was just looking for a rural town with Christian values and a deep sense of patriotism. Kelly filled the bill for the Brown family.

The other was a woman who a decade or so ago was fleeing the fast pace of metropolitan life in pursuit of a calmer, more pastoral lifestyle. For her it was sort of like the old sitcom *Green Acres*. But in addition to the Kelly green acreage, she also found herself deep in the heart of Little Green Men country.

Neither knew how the Little Green Men would impact their lives. And since both are doers, it should come as no surprise how much they have done to further the legend of the angry alien invaders ... in order to help their adopted hometown just outside Hopkinsville, Kentucky.

The Green Beret is Frank Brown, a battle-scarred veteran of more than 22 years of service. Like so many of his 5th Special Forces Group (Airborne) brethren, he decided to settle down in Christian County because of its close proximity to Fort Campbell and, of course, the Green Berets. He was on active duty at the time, but he knew he wanted to retire in this area, because of the special bonds of brotherhood of that legendary group of soldiers.

"When I retired, I had to have surgery on my neck. I'm a disabled veteran. I wanted to give back to the community that has supported me over the years," Brown explained, adding that 90 percent of his neck problem is "combat-related." No he wasn't shot, but he was injured while gallantly engaged in the rugged lifestyle and mission of his beloved Special Forces. The former soldier said that thanks to the support of the citizens of the United States, he was able to have a full career and raise his family. And when he did retire, his family was nicely settled in the green, green grass of Kelly.

And he had time on his hands.

The citizens of Kelly have reason to be glad that the place he settled into with this passion for giving back is their little village that never will be the same thanks to him.

As noted earlier, it was sort of like the old TV series *Green Acres* when Joann Smithey and her husband, Thomas, decided that city living was no place for them. No they weren't looking for a place to have a pet pig or anything. But they wouldn't mind a little livestock and laying hens.

Yep green acres in Christian County, Kentucky—the Kelly community, seven miles north of Hopkinsville, to be more specific—was the place to be, regardless of whether they got allergic smelling hay, as Eva Gabor sang in the old sitcom theme song.

Little did she know that she would end up spending her free time—when not farming and making candles and other crafts to sell along with the eggs and such at her country store—devoted to the Kelly Green Men.

How the Smitheys' search for a *Green Acres* existence led them to lives focused on celebrating Little Green Men is coincidence.

Or is it really? Who knows what is dictated out there beyond the stars, after all?

Joann and Thomas Smithey had looked around their home in Cape Coral, in busting-at-the-seams South Florida, and didn't like what they saw.

"I grew up in Florida and the hurricanes drove me here, but I needed to get out of cities. I don't like city life. I didn't like the effect it was having on my children. I wanted to do farming and livestock and let my children know a little about self-sufficiency."

The result of that goal is Joann's Country Farm Store, one of Kelly's landmarks, where her produce and eggs and crafts can be purchased.

Now, Joann and Thomas Smithey didn't know anything about Little Green Men when they sat in their South Florida digs to sort out the move that ended with them active in the annual observance of the 1955 Kelly incident, among the most-controversial UFO occurrences in world history.

"We just put a United States map on the wall and threw a dart. It landed on Hopkinsville."

Her story kind of makes a person wonder....Maybe the little men from outer space used the same trick when they decided to land their flying saucer near that farmhouse in Kelly more than a half-century ago. Doubters and skeptics have always asked, how in the world (literally) could space guys get the idea to descend on this little church-centered town?

The Smitheys eventually made the move to Hoptown, but within a short amount of time were making their home in the rural village made famous by the infamous Close Encounter of the Third Kind.

When they decided to put their roots down in Kelly, they were told by some folks they needed to look out for the Little Green Men, who terrorized the Sutton-Lankford farmhouse all those years ago.

Joann Smithey just laughed it off. She had no idea she'd soon be building a big part of her life around the alien encounter as co-chairperson of the Kelly Little Green Men Days Festival Committee.

The Green Beret named Brown similarly had little knowledge of Little Green Men when he went to the meeting of a neighborhood watch committee he had started in Kelly, as the first big step he was taking toward giving back.

"We had a community meeting where we talked about the neighborhood watch group," he recalls. "Obviously with anything, it takes a little bit of money.

"So we were kicking around some ideas of how to raise money. I said 'What is Kelly famous for?'"

In his mind he had the idea that there should be some sort of community festival to celebrate that famous thing.

He looked around the room. He reminded those assembled that "We've got the railroad tracks. We used to have a depot."

But, there really wasn't any big railroading event to tie a fest to. And certainly nothing like the famous bank robbery that nearby Guthrie, Kentucky, ties its annual celebration around—complete with a "deadly" shootout on Ewing Street (U.S. 41), outside the Longhurst General Store.

"Where oh where was Kelly's heart?" wondered Green Beret Brown. He at the time didn't realize that he was pushing open a door that many in Kelly had tried to keep closed. The most famous thing....

"Well, somebody mentioned the Little Green Men. I had heard of it, but I didn't know a lot about it.

"But then somebody told me the story and I said 'That's unique.'"

Obviously, this was the kind of event to anchor an old-fashioned country festival, said the affable fellow who had chased alligators as a kid and Osama bin Laden as an adult.

He learned further about a celebration of the alien invasion that Hopkinsville and Christian County tourism officials had put together a few years prior.

The Green Beret named Brown had missed that festival. "I was in Iraq or someplace," he said, noting his duty took him to Afghanistan, Iraq, Somalia, "and other places."

It was in Afghanistan, by the way, that he was among those soldiers interviewed by the famous author and Hopkinsville resident Robin Moore. Moore, who wrote *The Green Berets*, retired in Hopkinsville, living there several years until his death in 2008, so he could be around his beloved 5th Group.

Moore frequented the Green Beret clubhouse, tucked off a back road behind the Fort Campbell Army Post in South Christian County, to drink from his bottomless bottle of 20-year-old Scotch and relish in war stories. Brown, who does not drink, does not frequent that clubhouse. But it was Moore's book and the subsequent movie that inspired him to join the Green Berets.

"I saw that movie with John Wayne in it and I knew that's what I wanted to be," he said. "I wanted to be in the best."

The earlier Green Men festival, in August 2005, was staged by the Hopkinsville-Christian County Convention & Visitor's Bureau, in recognition of the 50th anniversary of the Kelly incident. It was the first-ever public observance of the Little Green Men, whose arrival in Western Kentucky was regarded as almost some sort of nasty voodoo by some residents. But the CVB—with the aid of the Hopkinsville Mayor's Office and other prominent citizens, scholars and socialites—turned that first celebration into a dandy.

The events were staged at the then-new Conference & Convention Center off Lovers Lane and at other facilities in Hopkinsville, which was the community to give credit to and cash in on the Green Men. But Kelly did not, as the townspeople really weren't involved in the inaugural festival. In fact, Brown learned that one of the fellows at that first meeting he held had gone to take the historical Green Men bus tour from Hopkinsville to the site of the attack in Kelly.... And ended up riding basically right by his own home.

"People paid $5 a person to get on a bus and ride on a bus to Kelly while someone (historian, Southern gentleman, educator and natty dresser William T. Turner) told them about the Green Men," Brown said. He figured that there was something wrong about a nearby city celebrating the aliens, but his own adopted hometown pretty much looking away from what he figured was a natural for marketing and fund-raising and community unity.

"I got to thinking, you know people will come out to see the festival here in Kelly and that could be a good way for the community to raise money," Brown explained.

"So we got busy and started planning the Little Green Men Days Festival. I figured we'd have 500 or 800 people out here and make it a nice little event, some sort of neighborhood block party."

He didn't know what he'd unleashed. He began getting telephone calls from all sorts of excited folks around Christian County who were impressed by the idea that instead of dismissing the Little Green Men story, the little town that was the site of the fierce gun-battle was going to embrace it.

That first Kelly celebration in 2011 drew 1,200 to 1,500.

"We were elbow-to-elbow," Brown reflected, happily, adding that the fest has grown steadily since, to the point where 3,000 people (or more, depending on the weather) is the minimum you'd expect.

And that's an almost "you ain't seen nothing yet" figure. "We expect 10,000 in for 2017," Brown stressed.

That will be the seventh observance of the Kelly incident … and it occurs on the same weekend as a rare total solar eclipse.

By then—Monday, August 21, 2017—the actual anniversary of the invasion as well as the eclipse day will be the final, dramatic day of a four-day festival.

Plans are not only to have activities but to allow campers—Green Men fans and eclipse enthusiasts—to pitch their tents and park their RVs around the soon-to-be-built community center and firehouse that will be the initial beneficiaries of the tourism money that Brown and company have brought into Kelly all in the guise of letting people have a good time and listen to what many regard as an "old ghost story."

The planning of the annual festival usually takes 11 months each year. "We take September off," Joann Smithey noted.

"Alien Stew," scores of vendors and exhibits, and lots of music are the staples of Little Green Men Days.

Tim Golden, who helped organize the very first Little Green Men Festival in 2005, displays a DVD on a historic panel discussion of eyewitnesses to the 1955 UFO incident. Golden was selling the DVDs at the 2013 festival.

The 2017 occurrence—with the 62nd anniversary of the invasion of the Little Green Men coming on the day when about 2 minutes and 40 seconds of total darkness will descend on Kelly due to the eclipse—has been years in the planning.

The timing of the two events could not have been kinder to the Kelly community.

"It (the eclipse) is the same day as the festival and the same day that the aliens are coming back," Joann Smithey explained.

Perhaps a slip of the tongue?

She means, of course, that it's the anniversary of the day the aliens landed and engaged in a gun battle with Lucky Sutton, J.C. Sutton and Billy Ray Taylor. ....

But her use of the "are"... as in "are coming back" ... points to a core belief that she has gained by talking to folks in the area, doing her Internet research, and getting to know members of the family engaged in that famous gun battle.

"We may not know exactly what happened that night, but we are determined to celebrate the occurrence," is the stated belief of the organizing committee that is using the milestone in history— the August 1955 attack of the aliens—as a good reason for an old-fashioned community heritage festival.

While she and other vendors sell their wares, and souvenir buttons and T-shirts are peddled to tourists, the highlight of each festival is a gospel competition named for Glennie Lankford, who back in 1955 claimed that a space creature was peeking into her bedroom window...Her scream helped launch one of the most intensive battles with aliens ever recorded. Or at least that's the story told by survivors of that night of terror.

Gunplay ...lots of it... ensued.....One blast from a shotgun even blew out the screen of Glennie's bedroom window.

Again, WHAT happened that night is really not that important...

"Our ultimate goal is to bring the community closer together," Joann Smithey stressed.

And that's true enough for Brown as well. Green Berets are trained not just for the most rigorous and dangerous duty in defense of their country. They also are trained to help communities rebuild, to leave them better than they found them. So, whether he admits it or not, the old Green Beret was able to use some of those community-building skills deep in the heart of Kelly.

Kelly, in addition to retired military and newcomers, is populated by many longtime residents who grew up with the alien encounter as part of their community folklore.

Although some outsiders openly scoff at the notion that Little Green Men landed in Kelly, neither Smithey nor Brown are among them.

"I've talked to Lonnie (Lonnie Lankford, one of the three survivors of those who were in the house that night), and I talked to Geraldine (Geraldine Sutton Stith, daughter of the late Elmer "Lucky" Sutton) at length about what her father told her," Smithey noted.

"And I've been talking to some of the people around here who remember that night and the military and the police here.

"All I can say is SOMETHING HAPPENED. What? I don't know. But I know the family. They aren't drinkers or storytellers.

"Something scared them to no end. Do I know what happened? It's a big Universe."

Joann Smithey said she's very familiar with the rumors and theories offered up over the years to explain the commotion at the Sutton-Lankford farmhouse.

She tends to get a bit defensive about those who attack the family. "We're a big military community. The first thing we do at every festival is The Pledge, followed by The National Anthem and an opening prayer.

"And then Geraldine takes the stage and gives the history of the Green Men as told to her by her father. There's real fear in her eyes. The fear has crossed the generation line. She hadn't been born yet when it happened.

"She says that up until her father passed away, he feared telling the story. He feared the nighttime. It always haunted him. That night was with him his whole life," Joann Smithey said.

As for Geraldine's uncle, Lonnie Lankford, he's always been hesitant to talk much about the incident, she said.

At the time of the Kelly incident, Lonnie Lankford was 12 years old. While the adults in the farmhouse supposedly battled the space creatures that night, Lonnie's mother, Glennie Lankford, hid him and his two younger siblings underneath a bed for safety.

When she talks about that attack, Smithey gets very animated. No, she isn't a full believer in the aliens, but she isn't ruling them out, either.

Brown is similar in belief.

"I'm a good Christian man, first and foremost," he said, explaining that he takes the words of his fellow human beings, including a very devout Glennie Lankford, seriously.

"I think there was something that scared the family that night," Brown said. "They wouldn't all have had the same story" if they hadn't all had the exact same experience. In other words, there wasn't time for anyone to make this stuff up.

"I don't know if it was Little Green Men, but they thought it was. If it's real to one person, it's real. If it's real in their mind, then it's real. And to that family that night, those Little Green Men were real."

Brown spent a lifetime chasing down and destroying the real demons of the world. So he's ready to embrace the Little Green Men, either real or imagined.

With that attitude, the town of Kelly now puts on the fund-raising festival to salute the bravery of the Suttons and Lankfords and their spot in history.

At the same time money coming in goes to help build up the community and to aid charity, like fund anti-bullying campaigns, a pet project of the Green Beret.

When it comes to putting on the Little Green Men Days Festival, everything has to be perfect.

Festival planners like Joann Smithey and Brown rely heavily on the reports of eyewitnesses and the newspapers of the day as well as the recollections of the various lawmen who investigated the case as they stage the event.

Those folks paint a clear picture of what happened that the festival planners try to imitate to perfection.

Brown, Joann Smithey and neighbors have taken great pains to try to simulate the original landing with a 38-foot, 2½-ton flying saucer that made its first appearance at the 2012 festival, where it was lighted up at 9 p.m. on Friday night and Saturday night. The saucer will glow for four nights at the 2017 festival, when the eclipse is observed.

"There are lights all around it and there's smoke that comes from beneath it like it's either landing or taking off," Joann Smithey explained.

"And we have alien figurines, stuffed aliens, standing at the base of the trap door that's there for the aliens to come out."

These are not just any stuffed figurines: They are carefully crafted duplicates of the space creatures described back in 1955, the same basic variety of space visitor that appeared in the film *E.T the Extra-Terrestrial.* Of course, the real aliens weren't content with Reese's Pieces and stuffed animals. For some reason, they apparently attacked the farmhouse, though no one got hurt.

When the conversation returned to the subject of doubters, Joann Smithey offered her viewpoint.

"Well, I've looked at some of the rumors that they have said it might have been. At one point they said it might have been horned owls. Owls have those big eyes like the aliens, but they aren't silver and they don't glow in the dark."

The theory that the elaborate attack was the work of escaped monkeys from a traveling circus really left her dumbfounded. "That's not basic primate behavior," she quipped, as if no further explanation was necessary.

Besides that, as most of us who have grown close to the case will tell you, monkeys don't wear silver suits. Owls don't either, apparently.

But there is a serious point that Brown, the veteran of missions in 27 different countries, likes to mention. Could the whole thing have been some sort of Fort Campbell-Cold War ploy gone awry? Or could it have had something to do with the arch-nemesis Russians?

Brown won't say what he thinks, but he does raise a legitimate point.

"It's interesting to note that Fort Campbell sent a major and some MPs and a large detachment of soldiers" after the alien reports began making their way around the county, he noted.

"They had all them soldiers get in line, arm's-width apart, and crisscross the area around the Sutton farm...."

Brown claimed that one witness has vowed that he saw that "some of the soldiers had found something and took it to the major and he had them put it in a Jeep and they left with what they found." Without sharing the finding with anyone else, including the hordes of lawmen and citizenry....

"For the military to have sent those people out, it's pretty impressive," said the 48-year-old former Green Beret. "There was something that struck their attention, wasn't there?"

Fact, fiction or somewhere in between, Joann Smithey said she gets excited whenever she thinks about the plans for the 2017 celebration—when tourists likely will pack Hopkinsville and the surrounding area, when concession stands at the festival will be plenty busy, and when the Glennie Lankford Outdoor Gospel Sing will have special significance.

"I still see something big as far as the festival that year," she predicted.

And there's no laughing when she's asked what she'll do if the darkness lifts in 2017 and aliens start coming out of the cornfields of Christian County, like so many dead baseball players, including Shoeless Joe Jackson, in Kevin Costner's *Field of Dreams*.

"We'll probably just say 'Hello' and let them into the alien costume contest," she joked. "We may not know if the aliens show up because there are so many people running around in costume anyway."

But how many of them are 2-3-foot tall? "We have a children's costume contest. We have a lot of 2-or-3-foot aliens running around all weekend."

When the time comes, if THEY do travel those millions of miles to return to Kelly....Well, why not show them some hospitality and let them take part in the festival that was named in their honor.

It may even be a chance for some of them to show off their pipes in the Glennie Lankford Outdoor Gospel Sing.

THE 'TRUE BELIEVERS'

While there are those who regard the events of August 21, 1955, as so much science fiction, perhaps caused by escaped monkeys, ornery owls, an angry cat, deliciously potent "Panther Juice" or even the emotional high after a church revival up at Kelly Holiness Church, there are also many who are true believers who will remain as such until their dying days.

Fact is, they likely will pass on the gospel of the Kelly invasion to their offspring. Those descendants then undoubtedly will swear well into the next millennium that some sort of beings in silver suits engaged in a gun battle—the battlers had guns, as far as we know the visitors were unarmed, though quite crafty when dodging bullets—during that fateful night in the generally quiet little village of Kelly, Kentucky.

These are the true believers, the disciples of Elmer "Lucky" Sutton and the rest, who really, really swear by the events.

Look up "True Believer" in *Merriam Webster*, and you come up with the factoid that the word combination first was used in 1820.

It should be noted that the authors of this book could not find any evidence of alien encounters back in 1820.

But going back thousands of years, there are tales of people who stare at the stars and wonder. That has led to the naming of the constellations being outlined up in the sky and to three very wise men hopping aboard their camels and following a big star to Bethlehem.

The latter, of course, are prototypical true believers.

124

So what is the definition? *1. A person who professes absolute belief in something; 2. A zealous supporter of a particular cause*

The dictionary folks go on to say: *It's impossible to argue with those true believers, as they think any counterevidence is proof of an evil conspiracy...*

Synonyms include: *Crusader, Fanatic, Ideologue, Militant, Partisan, Red Hot and Zealot.*

So, looking at those words from the dictionary and then thinking about those who preach the gospel of August 21, 1955, there is one name that immediately springs to mind as the truest believer: Geraldine Sutton Stith.

She is the daughter of gun-toting Elmer "Lucky" Sutton and over the years has become not only the protector of her pop's reputation but the defender of the entire Sutton-Lankford household who experienced the terror and wonder of that late-summer night in the cornfields and woods of the little railroad crossing/village seven miles outside Hopkinsville, Kentucky.

At last report, only three people survive who were privy to the events of that night, Lonnie Lankford and two of his younger siblings, one of whom refuses to talk about the incident to this day and the other unable to remember it. Lonnie's role and remembrances of that fateful night were discussed in an earlier chapter in this book.

In short, he was the one who not only professed true belief in what happened—based on what his mother, Glennie Lankford, told him—he backed it up by proclaiming that "Monkeys Don't Wear Silver Suits," a memorable phrase that has stayed with the authors during extensive research into what truly happened ... or did not happen .... in the pastoral town that now has 200 residents, if you don't count cattle and wailing cats.

Geraldine was not there that night. She was not even born until 1961. But she always has known something happened then, and she has presented her proof and viewpoint in a book published by AuthorHouse in 2007. It is titled, *Alien Legacy.*

The summary of *Alien Legacy*, posted on publisher AuthorHouse's Web page, pretty much tells it all.

Geraldine Sutton Stith recounts the story of the 1955 alien invasion in Kelly, Kentucky, for a crowd attending the third annual Little Green Men Days Festival in August 2013.

"August 21, 1955. Just another hot summer night like so many others in the small community of Kelly, Kentucky. Lucky Sutton along with his family and friends were enjoying a quiet peaceful evening. The family not knowing that all around them strange things were happening. Things that no one would come forward and talk about, too afraid to bring up what they had witnessed. But Lucky and his family were about to find out what could lurk in the darkness. The visitors were not from this earth. Were they possibly from the depths of hell? The gunshots and the screams could be heard by neighbors, but nobody came to help. Lucky and his family could only live as they could after the events of that night, fearing the unknown and wondering for the rest of their lives... Would they come back?"

Geraldine, an attractive middle-aged woman, has made a name for herself by not only writing this book, but by promoting it and winning over converts.

Annually, she has visited the Kelly Little Green Men Days Festival and pretty much kicked off the celebration by recounting parts of the book, which she wrote nearly four decades after hearing her father tell the story of the Kelly incident when she was a very young child.

She is not a boring speaker, either, describing the events as if she truly was there, as if for the moments on stage she has "become" Lucky Sutton and is speaking from his viewpoint, with the fear of the devil in her eyes.

"There was hysteria all over the place," she said back at the third annual Kelly Little Green Men Days Festival in the late summer of 2013, when she wore a white patterned blouse, jeans and sandals, with her toenails painted Kelly green. Those seven little words pretty much summed up her case: This deeply religious group of people would not have been stirred to such hysteria by monkeys or owls. What they saw were things from another world.

Geraldine grows very serious when she concludes her tale, adding that she wants all who she reaches to "Keep Kelly going. Keep it in your hearts."

Who knows, as her family has wondered for more than a half-century, if the aliens will make a return?

The authors caught up with Geraldine shortly after she'd left the stage on that steamy and overcast August 16, 2013, evening, grabbing a few minutes with her as she was en route to the booth where she was autographing and selling copies of her book.

She first apologized for the brevity of her stage performance, adding that she saves a longer presentation for "symposiums and stuff" about alien invaders.

But she's not at all apologetic when talking about the festival and her role in keeping the legend alive.

"I like it," she said, of the festival in general, adding "when they first came to me, they wanted my blessing" for doing the festival.

No blessing was necessary. She wanted to tell the story and she wanted to help the little town as well.

"It's really crazy. My family went through something traumatic in 1955…

"But it's going to help Kelly."

In other words, even if there are those who don't believe—and she is a smart woman and recognizes that those folks do exist—the festival designed to celebrate the alien invasion now is giving identity to the little town, raising money for a new firehouse, a community center with computer lab and GED training room and also helping the city rally around various charities.

The planners of the festival work 11 months of the year to put it together, and that alone has turned a population of farmers, retired Green Berets, preachers and country craftspeople into a close-knit community.

"If it wasn't for what my family went through, all of these good things wouldn't be happening," Geraldine said, watching as kids threw Frisbees, and steaming paper plates filled with funnel cakes and hot dogs were carted across the festival grounds.

Because the family was scared … and sometimes scorned to the point they felt shame about that night … it was not easy for her to actually learn the story in the first place.

As a child she knew something had happened. But what?

Her dad—who, according to the story, was the most-active of participants in the struggle for survival against the 12 or 15 Little Green Men—was mum for the most part.

Too many people likely had rolled their eyes and laughed at the proud family's tale of the 3-foot tall beings in silver suits (they really weren't green, remember) terrorizing the family home.

"They kept it from us kids for quite awhile," Geraldine recalls, noting that it wasn't until she was 7 or 8 and living on the family homestead, that some people came by wanting to talk to Lucky.

The visit brought the subject to the surface. The proud pop knew it would only be a matter of time before the kids learned about it.

So Lucky figured it was time to tell them about that battle that, according to friends, always put deadly fear in his eyes whenever that subject came up.

"He set us around in a circle on the floor and told us the story," Geraldine recalls. "You talk about one scared little girl.

"You could tell: He would completely change into a different person when talking about how they went through the alien invasion."

She said the tale made the kids—including her brother, Elmer Sutton Jr.—feel like they were "going to pee in their pants and run."

But they stuck it out and listened to the detailed presentation. Lucky, as noted, didn't like to talk about that night at all in public. Yet, he essentially comes off as a hero in all of the descriptions of the incident, whether he was fighting space creatures or—as some of the more religious have asserted—goblins from Hell. He got off plenty of shots, even if no alien bodies nor goblin guts were retrieved … at least officially (more on that later).

Lucky was tired of all of the talk about his family being a bunch of drunks, country-folk fueled by "Panther Juice," hallucinating about beings from another world.

So he told his kids, making sure his family's heroism—not its folly—lived on.

Geraldine takes the duty of being the proud carrier of the family torch very seriously, and that is what inspired her to scoff at the nasty little innuendo and set the record straight in *Alien Legacy*.

In fact, she noted to the authors of this book back when we visited her in August 2013, that she was working on an updated version of the book, complete with information that she had gained since the original book came out.

"I'll tell you one of them," she said, with a conspiratorial smile, when asked just what new stuff or tales she had to offer to reinforce public opinion that "Panther Juice" was not in play and that aliens indeed did fight ... perhaps even to the finish ... while Lucky blasted away at them.

"I had this guy come up to my house, knock on the door.

"He said, 'I need to tell you the Kelly story is real.'"

The man said that he had a friend who had been in the U.S. Military—likely the Army since Fort Campbell, among the world's largest Army installations, is just minutes away as the helicopter flies.

The mysterious visitor told Geraldine that his friend confided in him "on his deathbed."

"He said what happened was they (the Army ground troops called to the site) found the flying saucer that had three (dead) aliens in it and they had been shot. They were taken to Wright-Patterson (the Ohio Air Force Base where the remnants of the Roswell Close Encounter also have been stored, according to lore and legend)."

This version of the tale, as told by the dying serviceman, does add some fuel to one particular theory.

It is well-documented that the day after the invasion, soldiers from Fort Campbell were dispatched to the area around Kelly.

Just like their cohorts in law enforcement agencies from Christian County, they were looking for evidence.

But, according to some witnesses, the soldiers marched almost arm-in-arm, combing the ground—like lawmen searching for clues or body parts in a kidnapping case—as they slowly traversed Kelly's open fields.

More than one person has said that the soldiers stopped, loaded something into an officer's vehicle, and then took off.

Was that "something" a piece of a flying saucer with some Green Men carcasses?

Only folks out at Wright-Patterson and probably the Joint Chiefs and the various presidents know for sure.

It's not that Geraldine believes everyone. In fact, she has discounted the "slick boogers" who have come forward trying to capitalize on the family's trauma.

Sure, there are those who say this is a fantasy.

But look in her eyes and you know that in her mind it is history, not folklore.

"I can't doubt it because when you live with someone who saw those goblins, you have to think it was an alien encounter."

Kinfolk, and there are many in these hills, tend to support her words, although there are those who don't open doors to talk to strangers about it and who disavow their "Panther-Juice-tippling" predecessors.

Lynn Seats, who the authors encountered directing traffic at the CSX railroad crossing on Kelly Church Road during the 2013 festival, said she was a distant cousin of Lucky Sutton.

"I believe there was something out there. I believe in the aliens," she said, affirming her support of the survivors and their August 1955 tale of terror at the Sutton-Lankford farmhouse—perhaps 300 yards down Old Madisonville Road from where she was standing in her reflective poncho.

In fact, Lynn believes they have come back on more than one occasion.

"I've lived in Kelly most of my life, and to be honest, we seen stuff in the sky," she said.

Her basic story went like this: She was staying in the old game room and store on U.S. 41 (Madisonville Road), now torn down and replaced by a prefab Christian family life center or somesuch.

Out in the pastureland, she "seen colorful lights. And all the sudden the crickets stopped. You know how you always hear the crickets at night? It just stopped silent."

The authors already had heard a similar recollection of the night the crickets stopped chirping and the frogs stopped croaking from Lynn's aunt—Gail Cook.

A member of the Community Emergency Response Team (CERT)—a volunteer rescue squad—Lynn has seen more than lights. She also was a witness to a womanly shape, a spirit or alien of some sort, who would periodically appear and disappear out along the highway that passed by the game room.

"I think she was a woman. She was just covered in black. Couldn't see her face."

Her husband also witnessed that "woman," as have others who the authors have interviewed or just chatted up during our years of trying to give the incident its due treatment.

You may remember from earlier in this book that Lynn Seat's aunt, Gail Cook, had, back in the summer of 2005, told the authors that this creature in a black veil actually had been dropped off by the spacecraft and later disappeared ... perhaps after being picked up by its friends in the UFO.

While Seats is proud to tell her tale that so much echoes that of her aunt, she also is equally happy to see people coming to the town to either believe or dismiss the old story.

"They needed to be doing this years ago," she said. "It's a little, bitty town and this brings people in from all over the world."

During the 2013 festival, the authors—who were relaxing near the replica of the flying saucer—also encountered Seats' 17-year-old son, Brandon, who is kind of on the fence about whether he believes or not.

"I find it hard to believe," he said, as he walked along Old Madisonville Road, past the UFO display.

Then, he paused. "But my dad has hunted for the spot where it landed, and nothing grows there."

Others too have reported this barren spot out in the countryside at a ravine on the old Sutton-Lankford farm, very near to the site where the old farmhouse once stood. Fact is, Brandon said he wouldn't mind going out to see that spot for himself. It would be a good day out with his dad, he hoped.

And, pretty obvious by the look in his eyes, is the fact that if he actually saw that spot, he would believe in his family's legendary story.

Remember, the descendants of those who were in the farmhouse that night when the commotion erupted are pretty much split on the story. Some family members refuse to discuss it and even dismiss it as so much foolishness.

They refuse to talk to authors or reporters and seem to be embarrassed by all the fuss...or angry about what it has done to their lives.

Perhaps they'd benefit, as the authors did, by visiting with Marcum and Alma Brite, who were at the Little Green Men Days Festival in 2013.

The two were completely enthralled by Geraldine Sutton Stith's tale of the horrors and frenzy experienced by her dad, Lucky Sutton, and the rest on Kelly's night of nights.

The couple—"We're past 70," Alma allowed—had driven the 30 miles or so from Madisonville, Kentucky, to attend the annual festival.

They said they had heard about the festival before, but never made time to do it. And, after hearing what Geraldine had to say, the two swore that they would be back.

"Something definitely happened, but *WHAT* is everyone's own idea," said Alma, who was wearing the Little Green Men Days ball cap she'd purchased almost as soon as she and her husband made it to the festival grounds.

Maybe she bought it out of true belief. Or perhaps she bought it out of envy. You see, her husband, Marcum, was wearing his Roswell, New Mexico, UFO Museum souvenir ball cap.

Of course, Roswell, is the site of what is likely the most-reported UFO incident back on July 7, 1947.

No need to recount that tale again, but basically believers claim the government has for all these years been covering up a UFO landing out there in the desert.

Roswell was also, according to believers, the site of alien autopsies, also covered up by the government. And those alien bodies, so goes the story, are being stored at Wright-Patterson Air Force Base.... along with, maybe, the dead aliens and the saucer parts discovered in Kelly?

"We have visited Roswell, New Mexico," said Marcum, noting that the couple was just traveling through and ended up spending a couple of days studying the 1947 government cover-up.

"It's interesting," he said, pushing back the bill of his ball cap.

But no more interesting than what he'd found out about Kelly.

He said the evidence and testimony about aliens landing in Kelly was at least as compelling as that they'd collected at Roswell.

"Something really happened here in Kelly," Marcum Brite declared.

What he'd really like to see in his amateur UFO sleuthing is a Little Green Man. The Little Green Man may feel otherwise ...

"I haven't ever seen one of them, at least not yet," said Marcum. "If I did, I'd probably shoot at them."

Perhaps he's a better shot than Lucky and J.C. Sutton, Billy Ray Taylor and the rest of the boys.

Christian County Sheriff Livy Leavell Jr. (The "Livy" is short for Livingston, by the way) was with his fellow law enforcement comrades at the security and safety trailer near the entrance to the festival grounds on that summer day in 2013.

This practical man, a notorious straight-shooter as a public servant, was enjoying himself. And he would not discount the Little Green Men tale altogether. Not wise for a lifetime public servant, at the time in his second term as the county's top law enforcement officer.

"It's an interesting story, how it went down," said the sheriff.

He said he never had the pleasure of taking an emergency call to an alien invasion site.

But he wouldn't mind.

"I think anyone in law enforcement would like to get a call like that," he said, his eyes lighting up. Heck, it almost looked like he was ready to reach for his holster and go alien hunting.

The biggest believer, at least in physical stature, that the authors encountered out there at the 2013 festival was in truth a Big Green Man, who stood at a table next to the alien autopsy tent.

The table's contents had nothing to do with aliens, though. It was covered with paraphernalia celebrating ... and selling the U.S. Army.

That Big Green Man was Sgt. First Class John Wylie, 40.

He was an Army recruiter who was ending his 22 years of service at his favorite annual recruiting spot.

"I like it out here," the sergeant said, noting that he never missed an opportunity to come out to this festival to spread the word that Uncle Sam also needed people to dress in green... Army green rather than the bright green popularly used to depict the space invaders (who in reality had worn silver suits, remember).

The very next day after the authors spoke with him, Wylie was going back to Colorado to begin a career as a sheriff's deputy in his home county. But on this day he was giving out U.S. Army Frisbees and pens and other doodads.

After more than two decades spent in the military, including stints as an infantry medic in Somalia, Haiti and Desert Storm, he had seen the world's good, bad and ugly.

And being out here in this Kentucky pasture was a delightful diversion that he would remember for as long as he lived, a great way to end his military service on an upbeat note.

"I believe in it," he said, of the Green Men tale, as he watched a couple of kids throwing the U.S. Army Frisbees.

Like all U.S. military personnel, at least since 9/11, he had been exposed to so many horrible things in this world, vicious people, hate, violence.

If for no other reason, that gave him a good reason to believe in the tale that Little Green Men (in silver suits) had come calling on the Sutton-Lankford farmhouse back in August 1955.

The world he lived in and protected had produced Saddam Hussein, Osama bin Laden, jihadists and religious hate-mongers of all stripes. He had, as was his sworn duty, been fighting against those venomous forces for more than two decades.

As a medic, he had been responsible for patching up some of the results of that hatred.

With that in mind, the sergeant looked across the festival grounds.

He turned deadly serious and said he had one big reason to keep believing in the Little Green Men: "I don't want to believe we're the only life forms out there."

IMAGINE BUG-EYED ALIENS
(IT'S EASY IF YOU TRY)

When the authors—especially old Flapjacks who sometimes thinks he is communicating with long-dead Beatles leader John Lennon—listen to the song *"Nobody Told Me"* we can't help but think about Kelly and UFOs.

After all, it mentions UFOs in New York and Mr. Lennon tells the world he sure ain't surprised by it.

Be honest. Most of us likely didn't pay much attention to the mention of UFOs in the lyric the first hundred or so listenings.

Like most people who enjoyed *"Nobody Told Me"* from John Lennon's sadly masterful 1984 album, *Milk and Honey*—released by Yoko Ono four years after her husband's death—the song hit home with us for its focus on the pain-tinged rock vocal stylings, pointed commentary and sometimes outrageously joyful wordplay.

In short, it was typical John Lennon, the same guy who wrote about The Eggman and The Walrus, Strawberry Fields where nothing was real and Lucy in the Sky With Diamonds.

OK, well he also wrote about giving peace a chance, you know, and imagining a world where there's no war and Flap's favorite singalong, *"The Ballad of John and Yoko."* You see, Flap has always wanted to eat chocolate cake in a bag.

So in the song *"Nobody Told Me"* there is stuff about "Nazis in the bathroom right below the stairs" and "a little yellow idol north of Katmandu."

Perhaps John had seen some of these things in states of mind sober and otherwise.

But he swore he was stone-cold sober, although naked, when he really saw the UFO over New York City.

He also reportedly saw some strange creatures in the night during another incident.

But let's start with the naked icon and the flying saucer, or whatever you want to call it. The UFO sighting occurred outside his 52nd Street penthouse.

We have to go back to the 1970s and the turbulent days of "The Lost Weekend," when Yoko Ono sent John packing for 18 months so he could find himself, with the help of their assistant, May Pang.

May—who is a friend of The News Brothers ... at least on Facebook, although Rob has visited with her at a Beatles Fest or two—was John Lennon's girlfriend for that troubled time in his life.

She recounted the tale of John and the UFO in her 1983 book, *Loving John*. Over the years, she has repeated her terrific story in many magazine, newspaper and television interviews.

Again, remember, Yoko put John out while their relationship faltered. In order to keep John from getting too lonely, she pretty much assigned May the duty of being with John as his personal secretary ... and all that entails.

May and John Lennon claimed they had their UFO encounter on August 23, 1974.

Here is what supposedly happened that hot, summer night: The couple had just ordered some pizzas. While waiting on the pizza delivery man, a naked John Lennon was out on the terrace, catching a breeze, and May was inside a bedroom getting dressed. Suddenly, an excited John shouted for May to come out on the terrace. When she got to the terrace, there it was in the sky...., a large, circular object—shaped like a flattened cone and with a red light on top—coming toward them. Definitely a UFO.

Co-author Rob Dollar visits with May Pang in Nashville, Tennessee,
in August 2009. Ms. Pang was with ex-Beatle John Lennon when he saw a UFO
hovering near his New York City apartment in August 1974.

Fans or those interested in the 1955 incident in Kelly, Kentucky, may note that the spacecraft May Pang describes is eerily similar to the sketchy descriptions of the craft that carried the so-called Little Green Men to the Sutton-Lankford farm, where the notorious gun battle erupted and left either no body parts ... or, as has been reported by a mysterious ex-serviceman on his deathbed, a saucer filled with dead aliens.

Most who talk of the Kelly incident only reported bright lights and didn't describe any particular shape flying in the darkness over Kelly. So feel free to believe what you will. Whatever gets you through the night.

In the various published accounts of her story about the nude John and the alien spaceship, May Pang noted the UFO was about 17 stories above the street and made no sound.

At one point, the UFO reportedly disappeared, but then returned, and it was then that May claimed she and John grabbed a telescope and camera. Supposedly, the light was too bright and they couldn't make out details. Photos they took were overexposed....

Talk about overexposed! If Ms. Pang's version is the truth—and we've no reason to doubt it—then the naked Mr. Lennon allowed the aliens to get a pretty clear picture of the anatomy of male Earthlings.

The lovebirds called police, who said others in the Big Apple had reported it and told them to calm down. (We mean, the others reported the UFO sighting, not necessarily the gaunt, naked frame of the man the authors consider rock's greatest mind and voice.)

May was asked for further comment on the incident by the authors of this book, but there was no interview for us. Maybe the wires of her public relations machine got crossed or she's simply tired of talking about the UFO incident for the hundredth time.

We also asked if we could reprint the account straight from her fine *Loving John* book—a tome all Beatles fans should own—but she (through a spokesperson) politely declined our request. And that's quite all right, as at least she was kind enough to consider it.

Now, as previously mentioned, co-author Rob Dollar actually chatted with May, face-to-face, several years ago in Nashville, Tennessee.

The occasion was a "Fab Four" Beatles festival in August 2009 at The Mercy Lounge that was organized by Nashville Realtor Richard Courtney. By the way, Courtney is the co-author of *Come Together: The Business Wisdom of The Beatles* and a good friend of old Flapjacks.

A resident of New York City, May Pang attended the event to promote her other best-selling book, *Instamatic Karma: Photographs of John Lennon.*

Ringo Starr's former girlfriend, Nancy Andrews, a one-time model and accomplished photographer who lives in Nashville, was another special guest who was there to talk about her book, *A Dose of Rock of Rock 'n' Roll.*

Rob, who's always been known as a damn nice guy, bought an autographed copy of May's book that day, and a few years later, when he ran into Nancy at a charity event, he bought a copy of her book.

George Harrison's sister, who has lived in the American Midwest for about 50 years, was another headliner at the 2009 Beatles Fest in Nashville. Louise Harrison, these days, makes her living managing a Beatles tribute band that regularly plays the theaters and clubs in Branson, Missouri. (She'd actually been to Nashville for an earlier festival and—before he was considered too old or silly to be a newspaperman—Flap interviewed her and found her quite charming and lovingly protective of her late brother, George.)

At the festival at The Mercy Lounge, the two Beatle girlfriends joined Louise Harrison for a panel discussion that focused on their lives and memories during the heydays of The Beatles.

Now, Ringo and Nancy apparently never saw a UFO. And if George ever did, he never told his sister. To the best of Rob's memory (and he has a mind like a steel trap), the subject of UFOs never came up during the panel discussion. No one apparently asked about it, and the 1974 New York City UFO incident was one memory that May Pang just didn't share that particular day at the festival.

Of course, if Rob had known at the time that his future included a book about the Kelly Green Men, he for sure would have interrogated May about her Close Encounter of the Third Kind.

And, he probably also would have asked her if it was true that John Lennon once teased her about Little Green Men.

Legendary journalist Larry Kane, who has written several books on The Beatles, recounted the incident in his book, Lennon Revealed, which was published in September 2005.

According to Kane's account, when Yoko first tried to set John up with May and he appeared on her door-step, May told him to go back to the Dakota.

Before Lennon left, he reportedly quipped, *"Beware of little green men coming through your window,"* and a laughing May responded, *"Just go."*

While spending some quality time with May in Nashville, Rob asked her to share her most favorite memory of John Lennon.

"How can I tell you that when I lived with the man…There are quite a number of memories that I have with him. And, it's kind of hard to choose one," May responded.

"Maybe it's the one when he sat there and he wrote a song for me, and he played it to me. That meant a lot."

That song was *"Surprise Surprise (Sweet Bird of Paradox)."*

But getting back to the topic of this chapter: At the time of the UFO incident on the rooftop, John Lennon was working on his *Walls and Bridges* album. He made reference to his UFO experience in the liner notes to the album, writing, *"On the 23rd August 1974 at 9 o'clock I saw a U.F.O. - J.L."*

According to some Beatles lore—and it's never clear what is true and what is manufactured, as The Beatles were launched more than 50 years ago and Flap's old friend John has been dead for more than 33 years now, dammit —John also supposedly thought he'd been abducted by aliens sometime during his life when he was in Liverpool. Heck, it may have been with aliens and up among the diamond-like stars where he first met Lucy. You do remember Lucy, don't you?

Many of these incredible stories are out there in print or in television documentaries. Some are even plastered on Web sites. But, again, be careful about what you believe....especially if it's on the Internet. After all, things can get strange in cyberspace. Or, of course, in outer space if you are with aliens.

In any case, the UFO imagery doesn't just appear in *"Nobody Told Me."* It's also in the song *"Out of the Blue"* on the *Mind Games* album. Check out the lyrics if you don't believe us.

However, it should be noted that this particular song was recorded in sessions at New York's Record Plant in July and August of 1973, many months before the naked Close Encounter of the Third Kind on the roof.

John's interest in space, though, is noted in that he reportedly booked the Record Plant sessions under the name of "The Plastic U.F.Ono Band" rather than simply "Plastic Ono Band."

The authors have been reading about that song, *"Out of the Blue,"* and most of the critics of the day regarded the UFO in the song as an image for Yoko Ono, who captured John's heart by being very different from the other women in his life but did it as quickly as a spaceship coming at the speed of light.

We aren't song interpreters, though. So we'll just think that perhaps John was describing one of those encounters above Liverpool.

There's been much written, really, about John's UFO sighting in New York City, but the most fascinating account of Mr. Lennon's alien encounters is provided by his friend, psychic Uri Geller.

This story, too, has been widely circulated in a variety of media.

If Geller is to be believed, his friend, John Lennon, the great Beatle, told him of an actual physical, face-to-face encounter with aliens that occurred in the mid-1970s.

And they sound much like the aliens who the Sutton-Lankford gun-wielders described as appearing in Kelly back in August 1955.

According to Geller, who wrote about the incident in the UK's *The Daily Telegraph* newspaper in July 2004, Lennon told him the aliens had bug-like faces and left behind an egg-shaped object during a late-night visit to his New York City apartment.

Geller—remember he was the guy who bent silverware by playing some sort of Mind Games—claimed Lennon described the encounter while the two of them and Yoko were eating at a restaurant in New York City in 1975, shortly before the birth of the couple's son, Sean Lennon.

The Close Encounter of the Third Kind reportedly had occurred several months earlier after Yoko let John come home to their apartment in the Dakota.

Maybe the alien encounter happened…Maybe it didn't…

Although entertaining and fascinating, in all fairness, it should be pointed out that not everyone believes the tale of John Lennon being visited in the night by bug-like creatures.

May Pang, who remained close to John Lennon for years, even after he had returned to Yoko, apparently never heard the story.

There's good reason to believe that the ex-Beatle, known to love a good joke, may have pranked his friend, Uri Geller.

Only John Lennon, who, of course, is dead, knows for sure…Well, maybe Yoko, too, if she was part of the gag.

And, while old Flapjacks is a devout follower of the word as told by John Lennon, he admits that these four-bug-eyed insect-like beings, scuttling like roaches, could easily be John taking a swipe at his old mates, The Beatles. For everywhere John turned, after the demise of the group that was named as wordplay for the beetles (insects, like Buddy Holly's Crickets) and the beat of music, he was confronted by the beast that was that group. He never could escape The Fab Four. The history of that band that will forever be recalled as "John, Paul, George and Ringo"—in that order—was something that, like a swarm of cockroaches, refused to die and let him be simply John.

So we'll leave that one up to you. Whatever gets you through the night is all right with us.

Of course, we focus on John Lennon because of the details of his supposed Close Encounters, but there are many celebrities and wise men who have seen something out there, something they couldn't grasp.

We've all heard the government explain it all away as "swamp gas" or some sort of electro-magnetic field acting up.

Perhaps.

But it's a mighty big universe. If, as they say, God created this planet, then who's to say He didn't create another planet, another race, a place where evolution turned monkeys into bug-eyed creatures rather than old guys like Flap, that silly old man with a pony-tail, or Rob, in his businessman's attire with the occasional bag of Ferrell's hamburgers by his side?

All joking aside, the authors have studied accounts of UFO encounters and spoken to many people, particularly in regard to the Kelly incident.

It amazes us how much the night visions of the 20th Century's most-influential rock 'n' roller and peace advocate parallel the visions of Lucky Sutton and the Kelly gang.

Did a flying saucer descend from the night sky over that rural farm?

Did the Sutton-Lankford family and friends really see aliens in Kelly?

Did John Lennon see spaceships and later aliens?

All we know is that one and one and one is three.

Co-authors Tim Ghianni and Rob Dollar stand next to a display on the legendary
Kelly incident at the 2013 Little Green Men Days Festival in Kelly, Kentucky.
(Photo by Harrison McClary)

BACK TO THE FUTURE

Me 'n' old Death sat on a bench at Founders Square in downtown Hopkinsville, Kentucky, finishing up our morning coffee.

It was still hot. Boy was it still hot.

The News Brothers—Rob "Death" Dollar and me, Tim "Flapjacks" Ghianni—had been meeting out here on this bench every August to begin our usual run out to Kelly for the Little Green Men Days Festival.

And, only in recent years, we had begun selling and autographing copies of this great book for our fans at the annual celebration.

Our book, by the way, explores the enduring mystery of the Kelly UFO incident as we look into a crystal ball and imagine ourselves as characters in a book imagining themselves headed for a showdown in the future with the legendary Little Green Men who return to Earth during a total eclipse of the sun.

"Remember when that fat guy with the beard and tattoos took our picture right here on this bench back in 2013?" I asked Rob.

"Yeah, he told us he never misses the Green Men festival. I'll bet he's not missing this one either. That's for damn sure," Rob said. "Who knows who will be out there in Kelly this year?"

"Yep. Whatever, whoever. We're ready," I said, as I watched the bustle in the streets of the quaint city. A red Ford F-150, with 101st Airborne Division (Air Assault) Screaming Eagle decals on the tailgate, had rear-ended a bright orange Pizza & Wings on

Wheels food truck—obviously bound for the festival grounds—over on East Ninth Street near the Princess Theatre.

A bit of scraped paint and body damage. No one was hurt. Fact is, it seemed all parties—including the cop who answered the call—were in high spirits, laughing it up. Probably laughing at the fact the officer didn't drive a car to answer the call. He'd just walked out of Whistle Stop Donuts with a dozen cruller or jelly donuts and sprinted several blocks down East Ninth Street over to the wreck, stuffing the goodies into his face the entire way. It was an uncommonly good day here in Hoptown. I was just glad I was here with my best friend.

Things were getting pretty hectic in the downtown streets, with cars and people everywhere. It was so busy and crowded now that hardly anyone was paying much attention to Bird Dog, which made him bark that much louder.

"When no one pays attention to him, he just takes his lawn mower with him and goes over to Lee's Game Room to play some pool," said Rob, pointing in the general direction of the South Main Street joint where Bird Dog usually ended up anyway at the end of a day's barking.

"Why does he do that, anyway?" I asked.

"What?" Rob responded.

"Push a lawn mower around downtown all the time?"

"Shoot, man, I think he's just waiting to see if South Main Street sprouts grass."

We both laughed at that image in our heads. Bird Dog hadn't heard us, and we were glad. He was too busy barking at the top of his lungs.

Even though we'd been anxiously awaiting this day for years, neither of us old News Brothers seemed nervous at what might or might not happen in a matter of hours. After all, we had prepared the best we could by scouting out the Kelly area, even picking our spot to watch the eclipse … and whatever else might accompany it.

H-Hour—the launch time for The Biggest Show of 2017, when the Hopkinsville area would have some of the best seats in the entire world to watch a rare total eclipse of the sun—was fast approaching.

The "greatest" eclipse in "the path of totality"—the words the scientists and nerds and even our old friend Jim "Flash" Lindgren, a science-fiction apostle, used to describe the location where the cone-shaped shadow of the moon is closest to Earth—was going to be seen about 10 to 12 miles northwest of Hopkinsville off Princeton Road. And, of course, most of the eclipse-watchers were headed in that general direction.

But The News Brothers, always with a burning desire to be different, planned to watch this most spectacular spectacle from Kelly, where hundreds, maybe thousands, of true believers in the Little Green Men were camped out after enjoying the seventh annual Little Green Men Days festival.

Heck, it only made sense to us that Kelly—with its rolling hillsides of corn and soybeans and more than the occasional church or two—was the place to be on this most special day that we'd circled on our calendars years and years ago.

If the aliens were coming back—as this rare eclipse was happening exactly 62 years to the day of their first visit—then Kelly just HAD to be the place to be for those who wanted to greet them. After all, the little fellows already knew the community from top to bottom from their 1955 trip.

Not that much had changed. The old Sutton-Lankford farmhouse had been replaced by a double-wide trailer home. But the well where the attacked family got their water was still there near that double-wide. Joe's Garage, up Old Madisonville Road a bit from the alien invasion site, looked old enough to have been there at the time. And the Kelly Holiness Church still packed them in—including Sutton-Lankford kin—on Sundays and any other occasion of religious significance.

Over the years, Rob and I had been out to Kelly many times, attending the annual festival, of course, but also visiting with the people, spreading goodwill, doing research for this book ... and— most importantly—trying to figure out where we were going to wait for the big adventure. It had to be JUST THE RIGHT SPOT.

148

Rob looked at his Lone Ranger wrist watch. He had already told me that we needed to be at that "secret spot" in Kelly around 11:30 this morning in order to get ready for the show, which would begin at 11:56 a.m. CDT when a partial eclipse first would be visible. Of course that would be just the beginning of the drama. What would follow would answer our questions ... we hoped.

The total eclipse—about 2 minutes and 40 seconds of darkness—would begin at precisely 1:24 p.m.

"Old buddy, it's almost 10 o'clock," Rob reported. "We've got time to grab a quick breakfast at the Senior Citizens Center before we go out to Kelly."

Since I suspected Rob's watch hadn't worked in years, I got up from the bench, walked to the curb and glanced up the street to check the time on the historic town clock atop the old firehouse on East Ninth Street. It really was only 9:40, but I guess that's "almost 10" in Lone Ranger Time.

Still, my stomach agreed with the breakfast suggestion. "Hi-Yo Silver, Away!" I chirped at my old friend, who was flicking at his dead watch with his right index finger. "Let's go enjoy the daily special."

We knew breakfast was a special time at the Senior Citizens Center, and we were regulars. They'd be expecting us to use our regular table, where Rob had asked them always to keep an extra pepper shaker. I never could figure out the reason, because he doesn't use pepper. But he's my friend and I love him, so if an extra shaker makes him happy, so be it.

We slowly pushed ourselves up from the bench, collected our balance, and then we literally hopped and skipped across the street and climbed into Rob's Mustang convertible. With the top down, we both barked goodbye to Bird Dog and drove across town to dine with people of our own age who had stories—and lies—to tell to anyone who would take the time to listen.

"Hope they haven't finished up all the bacon," said Rob, who was known to enjoy putting a few extra slices in his shirt pocket.

"Me, I just hope the scrambled eggs are soft enough to chew," I said, playing my tongue across one of the many dental crowns in my mouth. "And I hope they have French toast today."

"I want my eggs staring right back at me," said Rob, who liked to shock people when he ordered what so-called "normal" people called "eggs, sunny-side up."

Just like at the senior centers where we always visited whenever we took a News Brothers excursion to other cities, the grub was pretty good at the Christian County Senior Citizens Center. And if you timed it right, you were rewarded with piping hot biscuits and fresh coffee.

Some of the folks at the center on West Seventh Street—particularly the older fellows, many of whom were Vietnam War veterans—sure had a knack for spinning some amazing yarns.

But the storytellers really paled in comparison to the tall tales told by our late and great friend, Okey "Skipper" Stepp, a former merchant marine who could put Forrest Gump to shame.

Skipper had traveled the globe and been everywhere—well, everywhere except for Hopkinsville and Kelly—before he settled down in nearby Clarksville, Tennessee. But, just like "The Hoptown Connection," he was somehow linked to anything and anyone of importance in the world. It was really uncanny.

Heck, old Skipper—who taught Rob the "eggs staring at me" line—once served spaghetti to Al Capone and lived to tell about it. He also was in his apartment overlooking Pearl Harbor when the Japanese attack started on December 7, 1941. Depending on the day you heard the story, he had as many as three ships shot out from under him during the war, once in the frosty waters of the North Atlantic. He'd even been a pal of movie cowboy Tom Mix.

Make no mistake about it, our friend had seen it all—all, except for Little Green Men.

Seems to me, though, I remember a "Lost Weekend" when Skipper mentioned something about seeing some "pink elephants" only a few years before he met his Maker and donated his arthritis-gnarled body to medical science.

While the Hoptown seniors talked in length about their great victories, their girly action and glorious adventures in and around what is now Ho Chi Minh City, none of them really recalled that we'd lost that war. Guess they were waiting for official word from Walter Cronkite. No matter. What really was surprising to me anyway is that none of them had any stories about Little Green Men ... although a few admitted they knew a thing or two about "Panther Juice."

One of the forgetful fellows came over to our table to borrow one of the pepper shakers, and Rob, a slight irritation in his voice, nodded OK, but gave him a cold stare. I thought there might be a fight, but the man brought the shaker back after coating the top of his scrambled eggs with a thick layer of black pepper.

During our pleasant breakfast, Rob and I laughed and told stories ourselves. We let it slip that we had high hopes of seeing some Little Green Men later in the day. One of the mean-spirited women snickered, rolled her eyes and then barked: "Damn idiots." She may have been related to Bird Dog, I don't know.

After the good-natured yakking ended and our breakfast had settled, Rob—as usual—surrendered his two pepper shakers to the cook, and I hollered, "I Am the Egg Man" as we sprinted out to the Mustang. Well, my own sprint was more like a painful limp, so Rob beat me to the car. Still, we both were able to vault over the doors and land squarely in the bucket seats just before Rob engaged the gear shift and "VROOM"—like a scene from a Hollywood picture show—we were speeding off toward Kelly.

But we only got as far as downtown and Ferrell's Snappy Service, where we were going to have them grill up two sacks of those famous hamburgers for later in the day.

"What do you want, hon?" the head waitress asked, with a customer-friendly smile. I gave her my typical order of a half-dozen burgers, plain. Rob asked for the same, but "with everything" on his burgers.

"Been a lot of people in here today," said the youngest of the three pleasant women behind the counter. "Most of them going out toward Princeton for the big eclipse, I think. Some to Kelly."

"Everybody stops at Ferrell's," the head waitress informed us, launching into a history lesson on one of Western Kentucky's most iconic old-time hamburger joints. "Yep. Been doing that since we opened here in Hoptown back in 1936."

I glanced over at the neon clock behind her that read, "Opened in 1929" and just shrugged.

While Rob and I were waiting, casually plopped down on two of the seven olive green stools at the counter, a big, black bus pulled up out front and a fellow with a drumstick behind each ear came into the front door.

"Hey, Steve," I said.

"Flap? What are you doing here?" asked the man, just before he ordered two-dozen "burgers with everything."

I knew Steve Gorman slightly, as he was the drummer for The Black Crowes. But he's also a fixture on sports radio in Nashville. Some say his sports radio work will become even more important to him than his stick work with the Crowes. What I didn't realize was that Steve grew up in Hopkinsville.

I explained that my best friend and I were going to check out the eclipse "and other mysteries."

"Wish I could do that," he said. "We've got a show tonight in Cincinnati. But whenever we are close, I have the bus stop at Ferrell's. The whole band loves these burgers. Even the vegetarians love Ferrell's."

Steve, an expert on Ferrell's, claimed there were people all over the world with that craving for Ferrell's hamburgers.

"There probably are even BEINGS out there not of this world who just have to have their Ferrell's hamburgers," he quipped.

Then, out of nowhere came the strange voice that only Rob and I could hear: "BRING THEM AND THEY WILL COME."

Of course, I just had to wink at Rob.

I chatted with Steve for a few more minutes as cradle-robber Mr. Death made eye contact with a lovely young girl, probably in her early 40s. Rob bowed, kissed her hand and handed her his calling card as we side-stepped our way out of the restaurant. You could tell she didn't want to let go of Rob's hand. Or was that vice versa? Anyway, it was pretty damn sweet.

Rob was so distracted that on our way out, he almost pushed me right into our favorite historian, William T. Turner—a genuinely nice fellow and dedicated man of history—as we darted from Ferrell's, which was started in either 1929 or 1936 and still made the best burgers in two states and half of another.

Mr. Turner, who's pretty sharp, already had guessed what we were up to, so he was kind of surprised to see us still in town. "Be careful driving out to Kelly," he said. "I've heard some talk about 'buses filled with foreigners' headed out 41."

With that piece of advice, he shook our hands and then headed into Ferrell's to order his own burgers. This time it was Rob's turn to lead the charge: "Hi-Yo Silver, Away!" With his shout, we vaulted into the Mustang like a couple of young action heroes. "Damn!" I yelled. "I think I broke my back. Tired of being an old man."

Rob snickered and turned the ignition key. "Maybe the Green Men can make you young again, Flap," he said, stomping on the gas. "Stranger things have happened, you know."

My loyal companion couldn't drive fast for very long, unfortunately. William T. Turner turned out not only to be the greatest historian we knew, he also was one heckuva traffic prognosticator. Traffic was horrible as we began climbing out of the Hopkinsville city limits and out into the countryside.

An old brown dog was able to amble across the road, navigating the traffic, with almost no fear of being run over.

An old woman, covered in black from head to toe, stood at roadside, selling apples and "I Love Green Men" bumper stickers. Something was off, in my head at least, as I continued to see that same old woman, selling apples and other souvenirs every mile or so on the way to Kelly. Course she could have outrun traffic. Who knows? I just know I was irritated by her because she must've been pretty ugly since she hid her face. And she sure smelled bad when she sold me our apples.

The drive to Kelly on U.S. 41, also known as Madisonville Road, was bumper to bumper. Made me wish I hadn't quit smoking somewhere between 15 and 30 years before.

At one point, Rob—frustrated by the lack of movement—decided to pull out into the oncoming lane and pass the tour bus in front of us.

But it turned out to be four tour buses. He found that out the hard way, when he passed the first only to see three more in front of it, all separated by only a couple of feet. He put the pedal to the metal and pushed the Mustang hard to pass all four of them.

"Hand me a burger, would you, Flap?" he asked, holding out his right hand, while his left hand worked the wheel. "I'm hungry again."

He then hollered: "Look at them! They're all Japanese."

Sure enough, all four buses were loaded with Japanese tourists, half of whom leaned out the left-side windows to snap pictures of the crazy Americans.

I guess we weren't the only ones wanting to High-Five the Little Green Men, who apparently have quite a following in the Land of the Rising Sun.

As Rob gunned the Mustang, I stood up in the car, propped my hip against the windshield frame, raised both arms in the air, peace symbols on both hands, and yelled: "Banzai!"

The Japanese tourists smiled at me, dropped their cameras and started bowing as we left them in the dust and motored toward Kelly.

Of course, no one on those buses, or anyone else for that matter, knew about our secret spot, where we would watch the total solar eclipse and wait for our Close Encounter of the Third Kind.

Rob and I smiled a knowing kind of smile. It was going to be a good day to see Little Green Men—and an eclipse of the sun, too.

This great moment in our lives had been a long time in coming. Looking back, it actually started in the late 1980s after The Gipper (aka Ronald Reagan), in his second term in the White House, was on the verge of decimating the Evil Empire and ending the Cold War. Older people will remember forever the day he stood in Berlin and said, *"Mr. Gorbachev: Tear down this wall."* Course I'm not talking about that particular speech.

The Reagan speech that caught my attention occurred three months later, and the only empire the president was referring to on this great day was the one that was headed by Darth Vader in George Lucas' *Star Wars* films.

Speaking before the United Nations in New York City in September 1987, President Reagan apparently adlibbed and added a few lines to his speech that sent shivers down my spine.

"In our obsession with antagonisms of the moment, we often forget how much unites all the members of humanity," the president said. *"Perhaps we need some outside, universal threat to make us recognize this common bond. I occasionally think how quickly our differences worldwide would vanish if we were facing an alien threat from outside of this world. And yet I ask...is not an alien force already among us?"*

Now, it was after this speech that the strange dreams began.....For years, I would have the same dream several nights every month....It would be in living color...I could see lush green everywhere...cornfields and soybean fields, some railroad tracks...a train...the steeple of a church...a bright light in the sky......Then, I would wake up in a cold sweat.

In early August 2005—only weeks after I visited with Lonnie Lankford and saw or MAYBE IMAGINED that strange, cigar-smoking man holding the cryptic sign in the shadow of the Lunatic Asylum—I began to hear the strange voices.

The words, always in a sinister whisper, seemed to come out of nowhere at all times of the day and night: "BRING THEM AND THEY WILL COME."

Then there would be silence.

"BRING THEM AND THEY WILL COME."

Now, as far as I knew at the time, no one else was having these dreams and hearing the voices except for me. So, I was getting scared. I know, I know: Everybody is looking at me, nodding and thinking "Those are flashbacks, Flap, you old hippie."

But these were more real than some *"Lucy in the Sky with Diamonds"* fairy-tale. I sweated out the dreams and continued to hear the voices. "BRING THEM AND THEY WILL COME."

I had absolutely no idea what the dreams meant or what the voices were trying to tell me, and I really believed I was going crazy. Of course, I felt better after I told myself not to worry because I was already crazy.

My dark period of stumbling alone through the World of the Unknown continued for years until I made an amazing discovery one day, only because I had started spending much more time with my best pal, Rob, during annual reunions of our notorious newspaper fraternity—The News Brothers.

On a sunny Spring day back in 2012, while eating flapjacks (the pancakes, not me) and talking trash about the upcoming solar eclipse, Rob confessed to me he was plenty scared about it, and life in general, because he had been having these strange dreams and hearing strange voices for many years.

"Flap, do you remember that old Kevin Costner movie, *Field of Dreams*, when he hears voices and follows the direction to build a ball diamond—"If you build it, he will come"—and Shoeless Joe Jackson and other ballplayers actually do come?

"Well, mine has nothing to do with baseball, but what I keep hearing is 'BRING THEM AND THEY WILL COME.'"

I about dropped my butter knife in my coffee. Then I told him of my own experiences.

Imagine our surprise when we compared notes and found we were having the same dreams and hearing the same voices with the same message.

Feeling a sense of relief, we put our heads together—it really didn't hurt that much—and managed to figure out this great mystery, using our smarts and great ability to solve crossword puzzles.

Some great power, much greater than us, was sending an invitation: The Little Green Men were returning to Kelly on August 21, 2017—the same day as the rare total eclipse of the sun.

And, apparently, Rob and I were invited to act as the official greeting party—armed, if need be, primed and prepared for whatever might happen on that fateful day.

I kept thinking about this, all the while wondering how both of us could be having the same dream all these years... hearing that same voice whispering the same creepy phrase.

But I wasn't worried. After all, if it was happening to Rob, too, then I wasn't crazy. Unless he was, as well. Comforting not to be alone, I suppose.

I was lost in these thoughts from the past as Rob honked his horn and hollered at some kids playing with sticks in one of the yards as we rolled, slowly, in the Mustang toward the little unincorporated town of 200 people.

That's 200 people when there's not a solar eclipse on the schedule at the same time that Kelly celebrates the alien invasion of August 21, 1955.

Back a second to the sticks. Have you ever driven through the countryside and noticed how many kids run around in their front yards playing with sticks? Well, around Kelly, there were so many yards of kids playing with sticks, you'd think they'd formed some sort of club or something.

But I digress.

Rob was a little antsy, because the time was fast approaching ... but the Mustang was pretty slow in approaching the site. We had figured we'd turn off U.S. 41, up on a hill and near the festival grounds, and cross the railroad tracks to get to Old Madisonville Road. In doing so, we would pass Kelly Holiness Church, where some of the Sutton-Lankford family worshiped ... and where a member of that extended brood which has populated towns from Hoptown to Kelly to Crofton to Madisonville ... still preaches.

At least that's what we'd been told by people who had no reason to lie.

As we entered Kelly, we turned right at Kelly Church Road where festival organizers religiously put up a banner every year promoting the Little Green Men Days Festival, which this year was extended from two to four days to take advantage of the interest in the eclipse ... and the mysterious possibilities tied in with the Green Men and their return ...

Folks from all around the country and world, not just the Japanese who were well behind us, stuck in traffic and clicking pictures of kids playing with sticks, were in Christian County for the eclipse.

Of course the international frenzy had started years earlier when it was announced that the Hopkinsville area was going to be among the most ideal places to watch the unusual total solar eclipse, a marvel by any measure.

Hotels and motels in Hopkinsville were booked years in advance. Many Hopkinsville residents were renting out extra bedrooms to make a few bucks from the tourists. Our friend, Rich Liebe, was among those renting out rooms in his house. But, not surprisingly, he was donating the money to charity.

The folks who were staying with Da Mayor actually were not only here for the eclipse, of course. They were "True Believers" to the core. Maybe even old pals of Da Mayor from an economic development trip to Japan taken during his years at City Hall.

For these out-of-towners, it was pretty hard to ignore the timing and the mysterious possibilities surrounding the legend of the Green Men who had visited 62 years before.

Rob thought of renting out a space in his house, too. Except he was afraid the guests would snore. "I hate people who snore," he said, by way of explanation.

Anyway, even from the intersection of U.S. 41 and Kelly Church Road, we could make out the festival grounds. But all we could see were the tops of the big tents and a couple of the carnival rides set up there—including a massive Ferris Wheel and a Tilt-A-Whirl on which the little carts that contained the passengers were all shaped like flying saucers.

We also could see plenty of smoke, from the barbecuing going on over at the festival. And we knew that campers were lining the field, as far as you could see, staying in pup tents, motor homes or just sleeping bags, having stayed out here—near the new park and community center—all weekend so they'd be in the right place at the RIGHT time, which was rapidly approaching.

We were getting close to our own Ground Zero, but there was a problem. A long train was clattering through town, northbound, and it was preventing us from crossing the railroad tracks that separate U.S. 41 from Old Madisonville Road.

Rob and I sat there for awhile, counting the grain bins and then the open box cars, as they crawled through downtown Kelly. The last half of the train was devoted to cars bearing the phrase "Ringling Brothers, Barnum & Bailey Circus: The Greatest Show on Earth."

The circus usually travels with its own engine, but there had been a problem down in Nashville, Tennessee, when a sudden hail storm caused significant damage to the engine—blowing out the windshield that protects the engineers—as well as knocking windows out on several of the cars in the circus train.

Nothing can stop the circus, you know. So while the engine was being repaired, the clowns and their brethren were hitched up to a CSX freight hauler to make it to their next show.

Acrobats, clowns, monkeys, horses, elephants ... Who knows who or what was looking at us as we watched the train clatter through? I noticed some of the busted- out windows were covered with cardboard.

"Did you see those monkeys, Flap?" Rob shouted in an excited voice.

"Yep. And, as far as I can tell, none are wearing silver suits," I quipped.

"Monkeys Don't Wear Silver Suits," Rob roared, with a big laugh.

Then, my buddy put on his thinking cap.

"Flap, they really ought to just go ahead and set up The Big Top right here in Kelly, because it's already turned into a circus," said Rob, reaching in his pocket for a slice of cold bacon, rolling it up, and sucking on it like a cigarette.

We were nervous. Boy were we nervous.

The time was short for us to get to our spot. Our secret place. The location we'd finally settled on after many visits to Kelly over the years. Fact is, once we'd found our final eclipse-watching location—actually not very far from the farm worked by the Sutton-Lankford family 62 years ago—we had secretly camped out there for two days, for two reasons.

We wanted to make sure that our secret spot remained secret. If we could camp out there and no one came to bother us, then we felt pretty secure.

The other reason, of course, was that we wanted to experience not only what we could see in the daytime at our spot. We wanted to see what was visible in the dead of night.

After all, for the crucial 2 minutes and 40 seconds of the eclipse, the short span of time that we'd been anticipating for years, almost building our lives around, it would be black as night here in Kelly later on this very day.

Anyway, right now, Rob was nervous, finally chewing up his bacon cigarette and rolling another one.

I kept patting at my sport coat pocket—I always wear sport coats when on News Brothers adventures—wishing that I had only dreamed that I'd quit smoking. It had been 15 or maybe even 30 years or so, but I could use a Merit 100 about now, I reckoned, my heart pumping as the last of the circus cars rolled past us, followed by a string of tanker cars and eventually a caboose.

Finally, Rob was able to nurse the Mustang over the railroad tracks, where we were greeted by an all-business, stern-faced man wearing a yellow vest. He was a member of the Community Emergency Response Team (CERT)—good-meaning volunteers who went to house fires, traffic accidents and baby-birthing emergencies—that always shows up at the annual festival to direct traffic.

After all, the money raised each year from Little Green Men Days is funneled into the community, funding projects like a firehouse, park and a community center with GED-tutoring room and computers for after-school studying.

And, of course, this year, with the confluence of events, it looked like a lot more money was coming in.

Back in 2011, when they first started this event, they had 1,500 people attend. In 2012, they had more than 3,000, according to festival organizer Frank Brown, our retired Green Beret friend.

And, other than a rain-spattered showing of a little less than that in 2013, the fest continued to grow over the years. It even was featured in tourism magazines across the country as a classic place for those traveling the country by car to visit on vacation.

This year, with the fest expanded to four days, with the eclipse and the Green Men both as draws, there were expected to be 15,000 people here, with tents and vans spread out over the pastureland. Some sort of redneck Bonnaroo, but instead of rock music and pot, there was gospel singing, Coke, hot dogs and a great concoction called "Alien Stew," but to me it tasted more like beef. I've put a lot of horrible and dangerous things in my mouth over the years, but I've never eaten an alien, so don't know really what they taste like. Probably like chicken, I suppose.

The CERT volunteer asked us what we were doing, since instead of driving straight onto the festival grounds to park, Rob was signaling to turn left onto Old Madisonville Road as we waited for the slow-moving traffic to get out of our way.

Rob, who didn't really want to answer that question since it could make us look suspicious, asked the guy if he wanted a Ferrell's hamburger.

He declined and cracked a slight smile.

"I'm glad we didn't have to give him a burger," Rob whispered to me. "I don't know how many we'll need for this mission. I hope we've got enough. And, I hope I did the right thing by having the ladies at Ferrell's put everything on them."

I nodded and patted at my old cigarette pocket again, waiting for traffic to clear so we could turn left, just up the road, onto Old Madisonville Road.

While we waited, Rob and I looked over at the festival grounds. Now that we'd gotten over the railroad tracks and as far as Kelly Holiness Church, we could see the giant spaceship that was created as a big draw for the fest. It apparently was based on a Bud Ledwith sketch that originated from a description provided by Billy Ray Taylor.

Course no one knows for sure how many spacemen—if any—came to Earth on a similar spaceship the night of the infamous alien invasion.

And, I guess no one really knows what the inside of the spaceship looked like. Perhaps we'd find out later in the day.

But the mock ship, a 2½-ton saucer that is 38 feet in diameter, was being touted as a spitting image of the one that supposedly landed near the Sutton-Lankford farmhouse. Of course, the original may have been much bigger if it really carried 12 to 15 of the Little Green Men, as some media reports have it.

Even at 2 or 3 feet tall, this ship would not have been large enough to carry the mess of little fellows from space. Even aliens can experience claustrophobia, you know. Or perhaps you don't. Or maybe you never thought of it.

I'm claustrophobic, so the idea of cramming into this small Frisbee-like steel thing and careening through the universe made my chest tighten.

It's at times like this, when I think of the tight fit of space travel, that I remember John Glenn, a friend of The News Brothers back in the old days. Or if he wasn't a friend, he should have been.

About 35 years ago, back when I was the associate editor and columnist for *The Leaf-Chronicle* newspaper in Clarksville, Tennessee—just down U.S. 41A from Hopkinsville—and Rob was my ace cops and courts reporter, John Glenn, the former Mercury astronaut, the first American to circle the globe, came to town on a Saturday campaign stop.

He was at the time exploring the possibility of running for president. Unfortunately—as far as Rob and I are concerned—he flopped on the national political stage.

Course he was far from a flop when it comes to being an American Hero (capital "H" intended).

Anyway, Rob and I actually shook hands with John Glenn, then a U.S. senator from Ohio, on the tarmac at Clarksville's Outlaw Field, shortly after he got off his plane. That's when this great man said words to me that remain immortal: *"To look out at this kind of creation out here and not believe in God is to me impossible ... It just strengthens my faith. I wish there were words to describe what it's like."*

Pretty good words about a few old News Brothers, don't you think? If there's one thing you can say about me and Rob and our friends, we make lasting impressions on people.

Hold it, Ghianni, there you go again, as The Gipper would say. Stretching the truth a bit. Those magnificent words actually were the iconic astronaut's musings to ground control.

162

I was replaying that glorious day with John Glenn when Rob nudged me.

"I heard it again," he said.

"BRING THEM AND THEY WILL COME."

"You hear it?"

"Yep," I said. "I heard it: You just said it."

"No, I mean the voice. THAT voice," Rob added.

Actually, I had been lost in thought, or lost in space, and hadn't heard it. What I did hear, while we were waiting to turn left from Kelly Church Road onto Old Madisonville Road, was the squealing of air brakes behind us as one of the tourist buses, loaded with Japanese, struggled to stop as it pulled into the congested traffic near Kelly Holiness Church and the festival grounds.

There was a light nudge on the back of the Mustang.

I gotta admit, I actually got angrier than Rob, and it was his car. I hoisted my old body out of the bucket seat and went back to see if there was any damage to Rob's bumper.

Rob, meanwhile, was getting his camera out so he could take pictures of the damage, I assumed.

But there wasn't any damage to the pretty silver car, so I calmed down.

The Japanese tourists also came off the bus to check out the potential damage. I guess they also figured they could walk the last few yards to the festival grounds and not have to sit on that stinking bus as it bumped its way through the traffic and the parking area.

"Banzai, brothers!" I said to the tourists, as I again flashed them the double peace signs.

Some of them bowed. Others smiled and flashed double peace signs back at me. Others took pictures of the undamaged bumper of Rob's silver car.

Rob, for his part, stood there and took pictures of the Japanese as they filed past. Some of them shot pictures of him as he shot pictures of them. Then the reporter from the almost-daily newspaper stumbled upon the scene and began taking pictures of Rob taking pictures of the Japanese taking pictures of him. Gotta admit, it was hard for me to focus, but it was a surreal if amusing moment for us which helped us ease our anxiety at running a little late for our special spot.

After the accident, Rob and I regained our composure, bowed to the Japanese and climbed back into the Mustang. We immediately turned left, from Kelly Church Road onto Old Madisonville Road and headed for our secret spot. The gravel turn-off was only a football field-and-a-half up the road.

"I feel happy as a monkey with a bushel of bananas," said Rob. Then, he added, with a hearty laugh, "Flap, old pal, it won't be long before we get this monkey off our backs."

At first, I really couldn't understand the reason he was laughing so hard at this time of imminent peril.

Sure, this was a great adventure. And it was great to do this with my best friend, just as we had gone on so many other adventures over the years—encountering not only John Glenn, but also The Lone Ranger, Tiny Tim and selected governors, senators, a president or two, Hollywood stuntmen, and crazed midgets—while attending everything from a carnival to a film festival to a funeral for Chico The Monkey.

Chico The Monkey...Now, there's another long, complicated story. Just suffice it to say that the death of a family's pet monkey back in our Clarksville newspaper days had always touched us. Of course, more than one person has claimed over the years that it was The News Brothers who were in desperate need of some touching and plenty of love.

But, anyway, as I listened to Rob monkey around... even though I was a little afraid of what might happen between now and 1:30 or so in the afternoon ... I just had to laugh.

And, of course, I roared after he tapped at his silly Lone Ranger watch again.

"Now it's working and I've got the right time," he said, goosing his Mustang a little as we traveled down the two-lane blacktop between the acres of 7 and 8-foot-tall corn stalks and the soybean fields.

"Hi-Yo Silver, Away!" he yelled as we whizzed past the entrance to our secret spot, after traveling about 150 yards, and continued down the road. "We have a little time. I just want to see something."

Another 150 or so yards later, we were even with 7650 Old Madisonville Road. This was the address of the old farmhouse where the Little Green Men legend was born, where Lucky Sutton blasted away at aliens with his shotgun while Glennie Lankford hid her younger kids under the bed.

The old Sutton-Lankford farm was long gone, and only the well from the old days remained on the property, which had several "No Trespassing" signs posted to ward off sightseers. About two dozen tents and a pair of small campers were on a nearby neighbor's lawn. Obviously there were a lot of people who had the same idea as we did about this magical day.

"Too bad the old farmhouse is gone," said Rob, who waved at a couple of kids who were dueling with sticks near the old well.

"You know that well is the only thing left from August 21, 1955," he stressed, pointing to the birdbath that is right by that deep water source now on the front lawn of the double-wide trailer residence.

"Yeah, I know," I told Rob, who apparently had forgotten we'd been here 50 times before.

Rob drove the Mustang past Joe's Garage, just up the road from the double-wide with the mysterious well. He kept going until we got to the next intersection—just a bit farther down the road—and then he did his celebratory "donut" with his car, slamming on the brakes and letting it spin around in the gravel until it was headed in the other direction.

The two bags of Ferrell's burgers by my feet turned over, spilling the tasty treats all over the floor mat.

"Way to go, Magnum, PI," I quipped to my old friend. He never would have risked gravel damage to his Mustang on any other day. But this was the day we'd been waiting for.

"Remember what the voice is telling us," I reminded Rob, as he tried to grab one of the hamburgers from the floorboard while I was scooping them back into the bag.

"BRING THEM AND THEY WILL COME," he repeated, handing the hamburger back to me. "Put it in the bag with the rest."

From there, the drama was pretty much over. We just had to slowly crunch on up the road, past the old doublewide and the mysterious well, go about 150 yards and we were there.

The entrance to our secret spot.

Before he made the left-hand turn onto the gravel road—really a path—that led deep back into the cornfields, Rob asked me to make sure I looked around.

"Don't want anyone following us," he said. "We need to do this alone. Or at least just the two of us."

I did a 360-degree scan. Behind us, the road was clear. Up ahead, no one was in sight. Not even any Japanese with cameras.

"Here we go, Flap. Hi-Yo Silver, Away!" Rob yelled, turning onto the gravel, one-car-width strip, a corn-farmer's access into his field of crops.

For us, though, this little road was our access into a field of dreams.

Like we had rehearsed on prior visits, Rob drove the Mustang well back into the cornfield, going perhaps a half-mile on the gravel road so no one could see us from the old highway.

It was almost 11:15 Lone Ranger Time—remember Rob's watch was working correctly again—and we needed to hurry.

Rob popped open the trunk of his car, so we each could rescue lawn chairs as well as binoculars and a small telescope. We didn't think we'd need them, but you never know just what you must have handy when you are in the eclipse-watching, alien-hunting game.

I grabbed the cooler filled with strawberry-flavored "ice water"—some people call it "Panther Juice"—and the old baseball bat I carried with me for protection. Again, we didn't expect violence and neither of us had guns. But a baseball bat could come in handy.

"You old fool," Rob laughed, some phlegm spewing from his mouth. "Remember Lucky couldn't hurt them with a shotgun, and you are thinking that you can hold them off with a Louisville Slugger."

"Well, I can use it for a cane if I need to," I said. My back was still sore from the times we'd jumped into the car and that often led to excruciating back spasms that would take me to the ground unless I had a cane ... or a baseball bat ... to prop me up.

"You old fool," said Rob, repeating himself. "Did you bring a bat for me?"

Actually I didn't have another bat. I did have one of those short-handled Army shovels with the point on the spade. I brought it in case we got stuck in the gravel and I needed to help dig the car wheels out to give them traction.

"I'll take that, Flap," said Rob.

We set up the chairs in the middle of the gravel road, in a spot where we had a full view of everything in front of us and above us. By the time we'd finished this, the steamy August sun had both of us pretty well baked.

But before we settled down in the chairs to drink the "Panther Juice," we went to get the bags of burgers as well as the apples I bought from the woman in the black dress.

The apples—Granny Whites, if I'm remembering correctly, which may or may not be the case—were for us to eat while we sweated out the wait.

The burgers? Well, we were just following orders. In short, they were a special order that had been placed "to go." And where they would go, well who knows?

"BRING THEM AND THEY WILL COME," roared the voice from nowhere. At least that's what I thought until I noticed that Rob was laughing. He'd heard that voice so many times over the years that now he had taken to imitating it.

"Don't joke about it, man," I said. But then again, I just had to laugh.

By 11:32, we were settled into our lawn chairs, eating apples and washing them down with "Panther Juice." Rob had found another slice of bacon in his pocket, so he was chewing on that as well.

We also put on our sunglasses, with their sun-shielding lenses. We knew, you aren't supposed to stare into the sun during an eclipse. But warnings be damned on this day.

Twenty-four minutes later, precisely at 11:56, a dark slit appeared on the edge of the sun and Rob reached for another apple.

It was the beginning of the partial eclipse.

At first there was stillness in the tepid August air. But the wind began to build slightly as the sun became increasingly darkened by the moon's shadow.

"I'm being followed by a moon shadow, moon shadow, moon shadow," I sang Cat Stevens' old song, softly and very poorly. Sometimes when I'm nervous I sing whatever pops into my head.

An owl hooted off in the growing darkness. It was answered by another, which is normal, of course, as they travel in pairs.

"Shhh," said Rob, who threw the core of the apple into the cornfield. I didn't know if he was shushing me or the owls.

We sat there enjoying the partial eclipse for the next hour and 28 minutes, as the sun slowly disappeared behind the moon and the bright and hot August day became dark and slightly cooler, because the sun wasn't beating down on us.

"BRING THEM AND THEY WILL COME," Rob whispered, handing me one of the bags of burgers we'd been toting around most of the day.

At that very moment, I thought I saw something flash across the darkening sky.

"Did you see that?" I asked Rob, who had his face buried in his Ferrell's bag, enjoying the aroma of the burgers.

"See what?" he responded, looking out into the cornfield.

We didn't know what might happen or if anything truly would come out of the cornfield on this 62nd anniversary of the Little Green Men's battle with Glennie and the kids.

But it just seemed too much of a sure thing that if something did happen, it would be during the total eclipse of the sun.

I heard Rob crinkle the paper of one of the burgers in his bag at about 1:20 p.m., with total darkness just minutes away. I

168

followed suit and also unwrapped one of the burgers, trying to let the aroma spread through the near darkness.

At 1:24, just as total darkness swallowed us, we heard cheers from the festival grounds just down the road. A couple of dogs barked somewhere out in the cornfield.

Then, Rob and I heard a rustle near us from a part of the cornfield to our right. Then another, louder, to our left. I thought I saw a silver glint.

Rob pointed down the gravel road toward some sort of reflection that quickly disappeared into the cornfield. Then there was another one...And another one...There were silver glints everywhere...All moving toward us...

"Flap!" hollered Rob. "Get your hamburgers ready...."

I also grabbed my baseball bat, just in case, and handed him the little shovel as the sounds of the rustling in the cornfield seemed to be building to the point where we could hear it clearly even though the Japanese tourists up at the festival grounds and other Green Men celebrants were cheering, screaming and laughing, like kids on a roller-coaster.

"Do you think they ate Ferrell's when they were here in 1955?" Rob asked as he got himself into position.

There was no time to answer my old pal. The rustling of the cornstalks was now occurring at a maddening pace.

There was some time—maybe a few seconds—to think the unthinkable... and put on my brave face. As I stiffened my upper lip, I was startled by a familiar voice from the happiest days of my childhood. It came from somewhere out in the cornfield.

"Timmy, throw some of those burgers out here for me and my little friends," snarled someone, or maybe "something" not of this world—if I was falling prey to an alien trick. "Treat us right....Thank you very much."

The time had come for Rob and I to Take Care of Business. Of course, I had to wonder, "ELVIS, WHERE YOU BEEN?"

Not really expecting an answer, I nervously smiled and whispered to myself something I knew for sure was true, "MONKEYS DON'T WEAR SILVER SUITS! ....But Elvis and aliens sure do....."

It was up to me to Tweet this most important message to the world, so I started to pray to God for enough time to perform my divine mission.

After my prayer, Rob and I both held the hamburger bags at arm's-length, our sacrificial offering to the unknown.

"Whatever happens, no one's ever going to believe us," Rob muttered.

It was hot. Boy was it hot.

And then, just like a lost and confused hound dog, the wind began to howl.

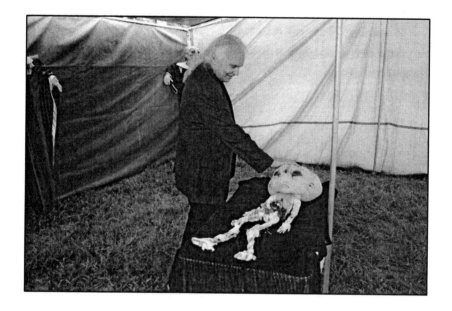

If Kelly expert Isabel Davis actually had an alien as evidence, it would have made for a much easier exploration. Here, co-author Tim Ghianni delivers the "last rites" to a Little Green Man in the Alien Autopsy attraction at the annual festival in Kelly.

ACKNOWLEDGMENTS

This book was never intended to prove, or disprove, the story that a flying saucer landed in Kelly, Kentucky, on August 21, 1955, and little men from outer space visited a night of terror upon the 11 occupants of a farmhouse.

Because so much time already has elapsed, it's doubtful anyone will ever be able to step forward and provide an explanation that finally puts the matter to rest.

And, of course, that's the beauty of the Kelly Green Men case. Imagination will forever run parallel to reason in the examination of this legendary Close Encounter of the Third Kind.

The authors could not have pursued and completed a project of this magnitude without the assistance and encouragement from so many friends and supporters.

At the top of the list is the J. Allen Hynek Center for UFO Studies (CUFOS) in Chicago, Illinois, and its scientific director, Dr. Mark Rodeghier.

In 1978, CUFOS published *Close Encounter at Kelly and Others of 1955*, a 196-page scientific study that was co-written by Isabel Davis & Ted Bloecher.

Most of this publication centered on a field investigation undertaken by Isabel Davis in the summer of 1956—less than a year after the Kelly incident. To this day, Davis' work is regarded as probably the timeliest and most thorough and comprehensive independent investigation of the Kelly case.

CUFOS granted the authors permission to freely use the Davis publication as one of our references, and for this, we are truly grateful. It was invaluable in our efforts to tell the entire story, particularly since many of the original eyewitnesses are no longer living.

We want to thank the surviving members of the Sutton-Lankford family for sharing their memories in recent years, something that most certainly was difficult for them after unfairly suffering decades of public ridicule. A special thank-you is in order for Lonnie Lankford, who befriended us in our work and warmly invited us into his home.

The good people of Hopkinsville, Kentucky, and Kelly, Kentucky, also are most deserving of a pat on the back for always making us feel welcome while we worked on this book. We particularly wish to single out for praise local historian William T. Turner and the Christian County Historical Society, Cheryl Cook of the Hopkinsville-Christian County Convention & Visitor's Bureau, Tim Golden, Steve "Bird Dog" Page, the staff of the Pennyroyal Area Museum, the kind folks at Ferrell's Snappy Service, and Kelly community leaders Frank Brown and Joann Smithey.

George McCouch, longtime circulation manager for the *Kentucky New Era* newspaper, is another person most deserving of special recognition. He was among the earliest proponents of a festival to commemorate the Kelly Green Men incident, realizing the economic impact and opportunities for Christian County. Sadly, and so ironically, George passed away after a long illness in mid-December of last year, just as this book that he surely would have loved was on its way to the presses.

Finally, we want to recognize and give credit to our former newspaper employers—the *Kentucky New Era* in Hopkinsville, Kentucky, and *The Tennessean* in Nashville, Tennessee—for allowing us the opportunity over the years to research and write stories about one of the most fascinating UFO cases in history.

REFERENCES

Isabel Davis & Ted Bloecher, *Close Encounter at Kelly and Others of 1955*, The J. Allen Hynek Center for UFO Studies (CUFOS), Chicago, Illinois, (1978), Source in Chapters 2, 3, 4, and 11

Close Encounters of the Third Kind, Columbia Pictures, Los Angeles, California, (November 1977), Chapters 5, 8

Entertainment Weekly magazine, "Steven Spielberg: The ET Interview," (December 9, 2011), Source in Chapter 5

E.T. the Extra-terrestrial, Universal Pictures, Los Angeles, California, (June 1982), Chapters 1, 5, 6, 7, 8, and 12

Field of Dreams, Universal Pictures, Los Angeles, California, (April 1989), Chapters 12, 15

Gomer Pyle, U.S.M.C., CBS television sitcom, (1964-1969), Chapter 2

Green Acres, CBS television sitcom, (1965-1971), Chapters 1, 12

"Heartlight," Song written by Neil Diamond, Carol Bayer Sager and Burt Bacharach, Columbia Records, New York City, New York, (1982), Chapter 7

The J. Allen Hynek Center for UFO Studies (CUFOS), Chicago, Illinois, Web site, http://www.cufos.org/, Source in Chapter 8

Tim Golden, Golden Video Productions, Hopkinsville, Kentucky, Kelly Green Men Festival DVD, "Panel Discussion August 20, 2005," (August 2005), Chapters 9, 10, 11

Indiana Jones and the Kingdom of the Crystal Skull, Paramount Pictures Corp., Hollywood, California, (May 2008), Chapter 11

Interviews (July 2005) Lonnie Lankford, R.N. Ferguson, William T. Turner, Cheryl Cook, Gail Cook, David Brasher, Wendell McCord, Linda Renshaw, Rachel Greenwell, Greg Little, Frank Dudas, Jim Fleming, Mike Lackey, and Norma Malone; (August 2013) Geraldine Sutton Stith, Lynn Seats, Brandon Seats, Tim Golden, Livy Leavell Jr., Frank Brown, Joann Smithey, Marcum Brite, Alma Brite, and John Wylie

Larry Kane, *Lennon Revealed*, Running Press, Philadelphia, Pennsylvania, (2005), Chapter 14

Kentucky New Era newspaper, Hopkinsville, Kentucky, August 22, 1955, edition (Chapters 2, 3), September 11, 1957, edition (Chapter 3), August 18-20, 1955, editions (Chapters 4, 11), March 17, 1981, edition (Chapters 2, 10), August 24, 2001, edition (Chapters 6, 9), and August 18, 2005, edition (Chapter 9)

Renault Leclet, "What is the Real Nature of the Kelly-Hopkinsville Entities?" http://francine.juncosa.club.fr/pages/souspagekelly3eng.htm, (August 2001), Retrieved August 5, 2005, Source in Chapters 2, 3, 9, 11

Yann Mege, "Kelly: la nuit des extraterrestres." *Phénoména*, N°45, (June 2001), Source in Chapters 2, 3, 11

My Favorite Martian, CBS television sitcom, (1963-1966), Chapter 6

Dr. Joe Nickell, "Siege of Little Green Men: The 1955 Kelly, Kentucky, Incident," Volume 30.6, *Skeptical Inquirer* science magazine, (November/December 2006), Retrieved from Committee for Skeptical Inquiry Web site, http://www.csicop.org, December 11, 2006, Source in Chapters 9, 11

May Pang, *Loving John*, Warner Books, New York City, New York, (1983), Chapter 14

Project Blue Book Archive Supporting Serious UFO Research, Web site, http://bluebookarchive.org, Retrieved September 24, 2013, Source in Chapter 3

David L. Riley, "The Kelly Green Men," Research Paper, Presented to the Christian County Historical Society, (1985), Source in Chapters 2, 10

Jacqueline Sanders, "Panic in Kentucky," *The Saucerian Review*, Gray Barker, Clarksburg, West Virginia, (January 1956), Source in Chapters 6, 11

Signs, Touchstone Pictures, Burbank, California, (August 2002), Chapter 7

Geraldine Sutton Stith, *Alien Legacy*, AuthorHouse, Bloomington, Indiana, (2007), Chapter 13

Ron Sydnor, "The Kelly Incident," Poem, (May 27, 2004), Chapter 9

The Beatles (John Lennon, Paul McCartney, George Harrison and Ringo Starr), Albums cited (*Milk and Honey, Mind Games,* and *Walls and Bridges*), Chapter 14, Songs cited ("*Lucy in the Sky with Diamonds," "Nobody Told Me," "Out of the Blue," "Surprise Surprise (Sweet Bird of Paradox)," and "The Ballad of John and Yoko"*), Chapters 14, 15

The Daily Telegraph, London, England, "The Night Aliens Called on Lennon (Account By Uri Geller)," (July 12, 2004), Retrieved from UFO Evidence Web site, http://www.ufoevidence.org, September 1, 2013, Chapter 14

The Tennessean newspaper, Nashville, Tennessee, Life magazine, *Sunday Tennessean,* August 7, 2005, Source in Chapters 4, 6, 7, 8, 10, 11

Topps Comics, *The X-Files,* "Crop Duster," Volume 1, No. 32, (August 1997), Source in Chapter 5

UFO Universe magazine, Jacqueline Sanders, "An On-The-Spot Investigation: The Hopkinsville Case—Terror in Kentucky," (Winter 1994 Edition), Source in Chapters 6, 11

2001: A Space Odyssey, Metro-Goldwyn-Mayer Studios Inc., Beverly Hills, California, (April 1968), Chapter 6